HAWAII

PHOTOGRAPHS BY ELIZABETH KRAMER

THIS IS PART OF THE VISITING SERIES.

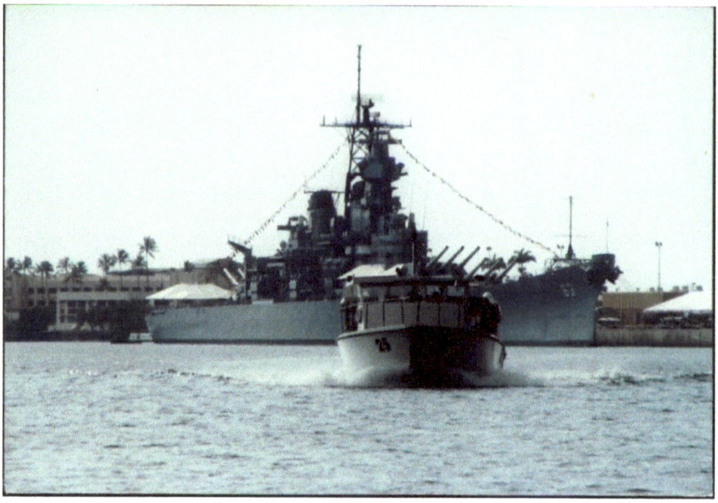

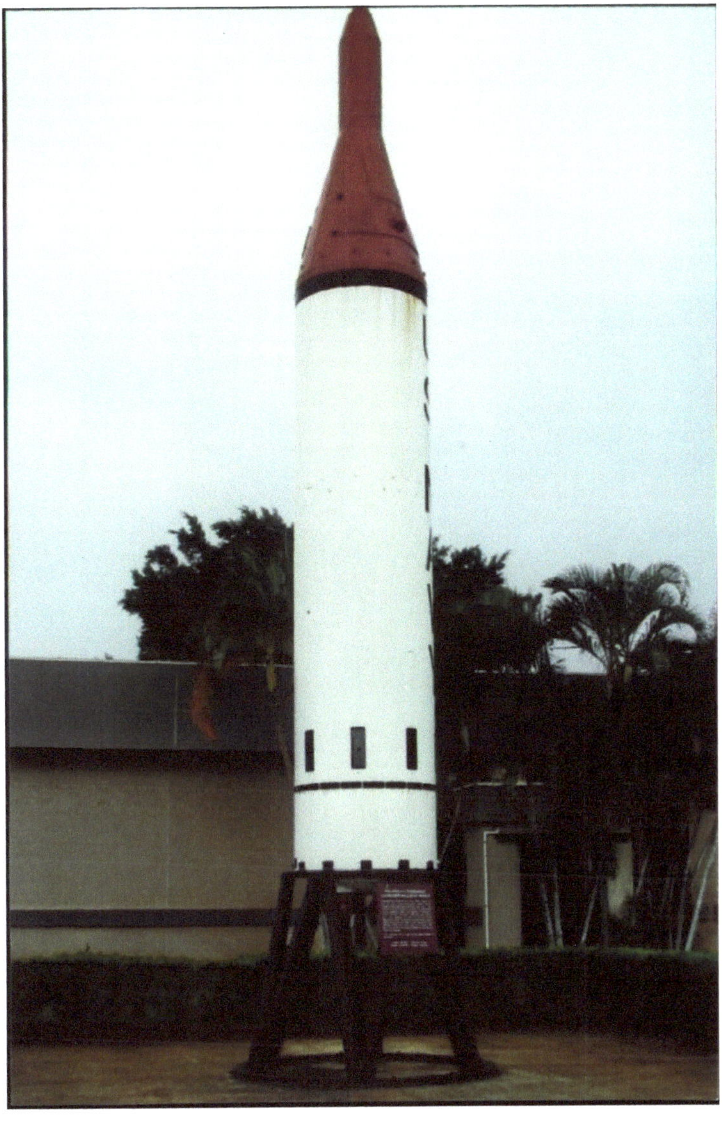

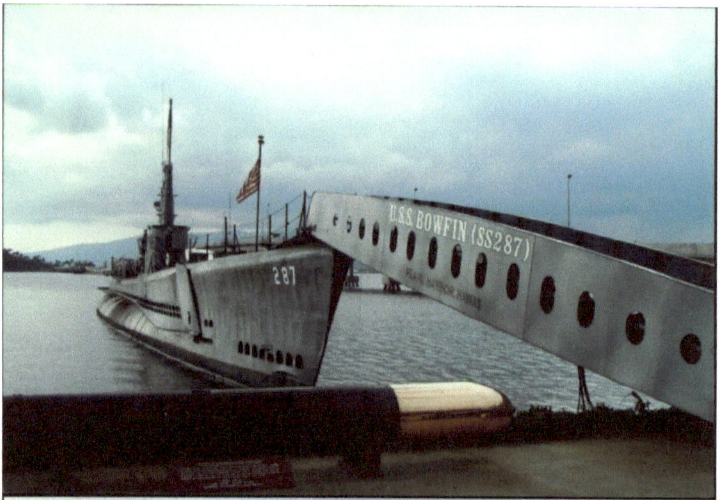
U.S.S. BOWFIN (SS287)
287

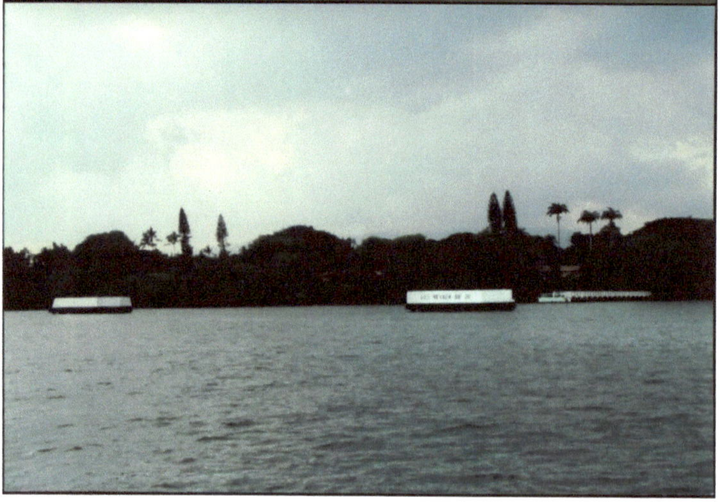

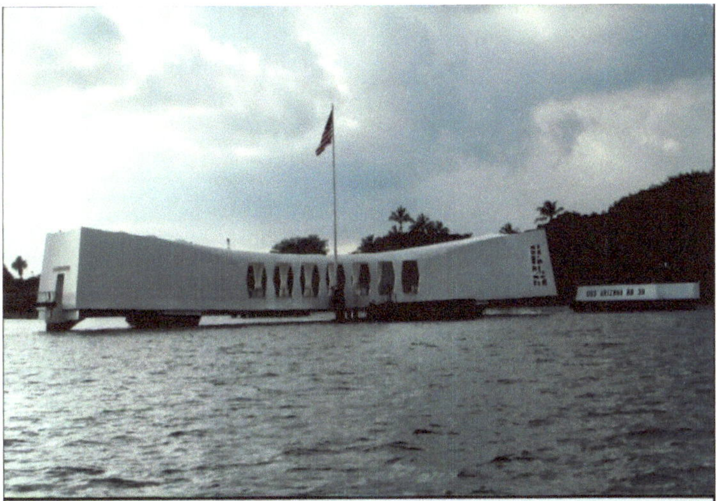
USS ARIZONA BB 39

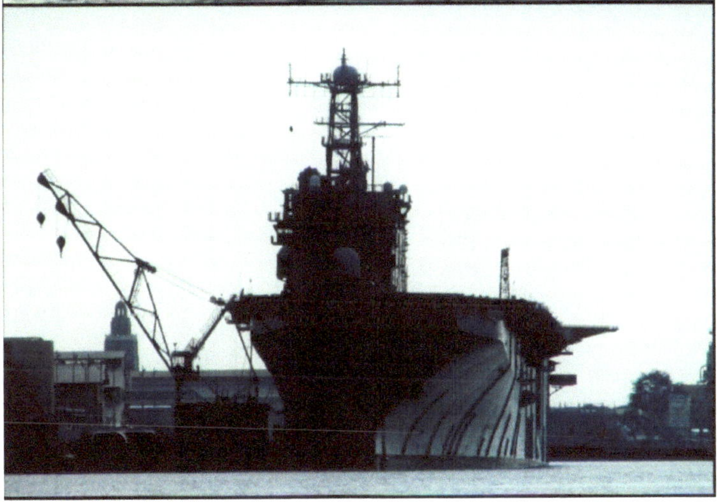

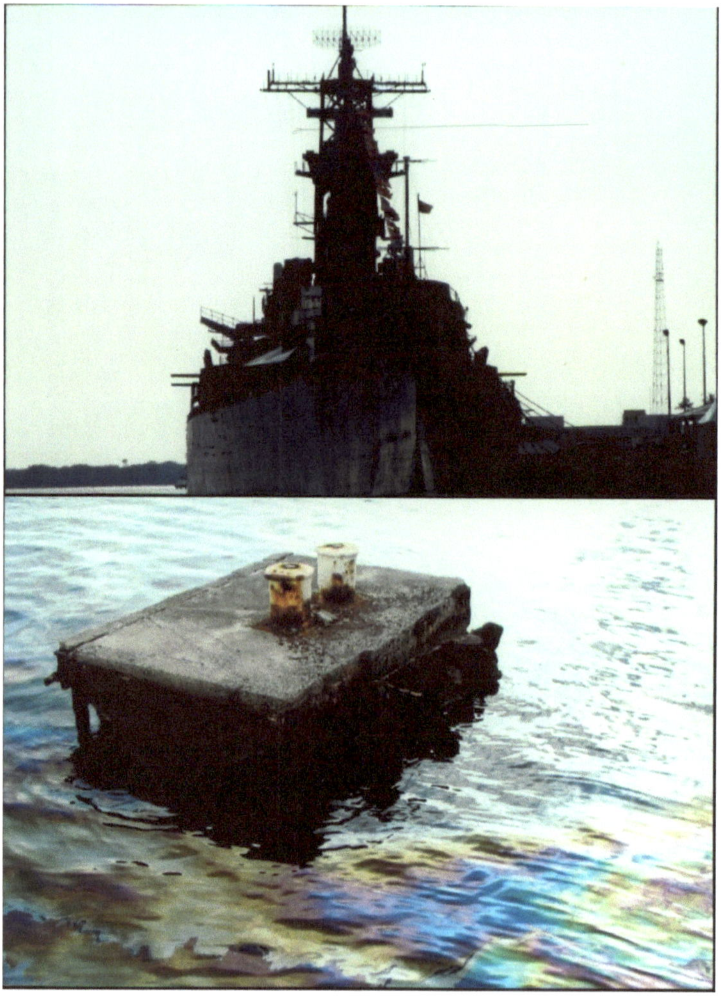

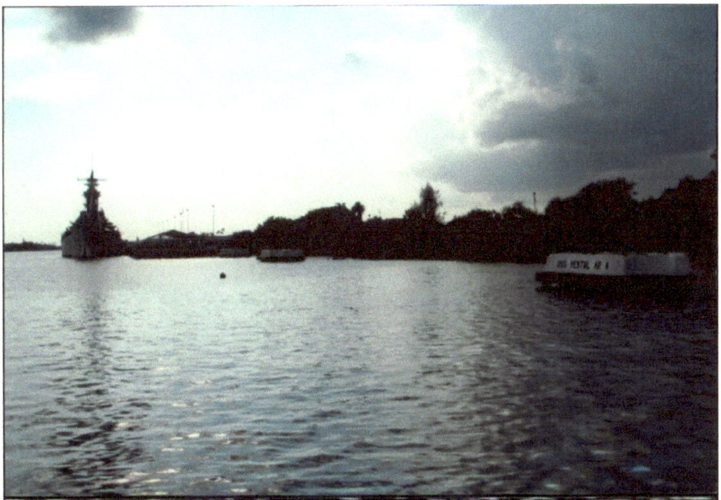

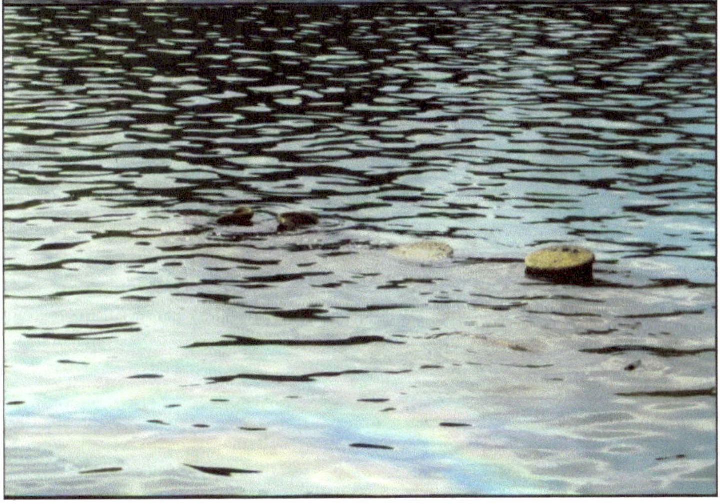

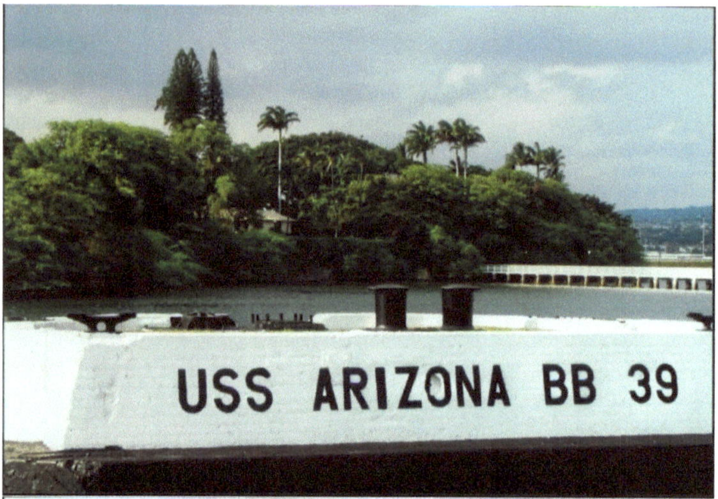
USS ARIZONA BB 39

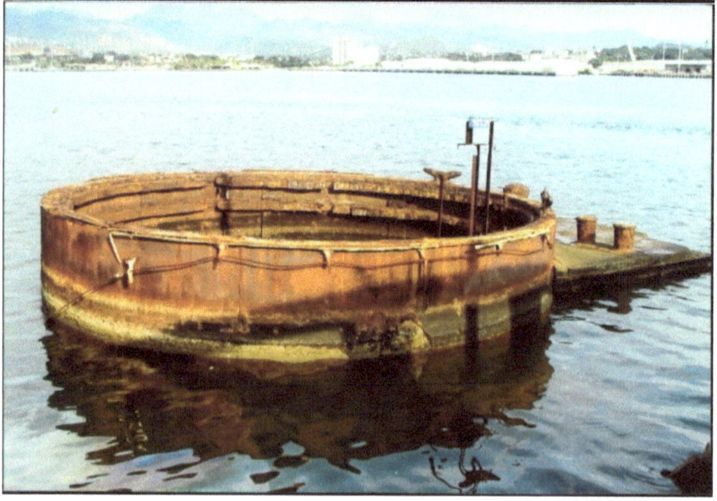

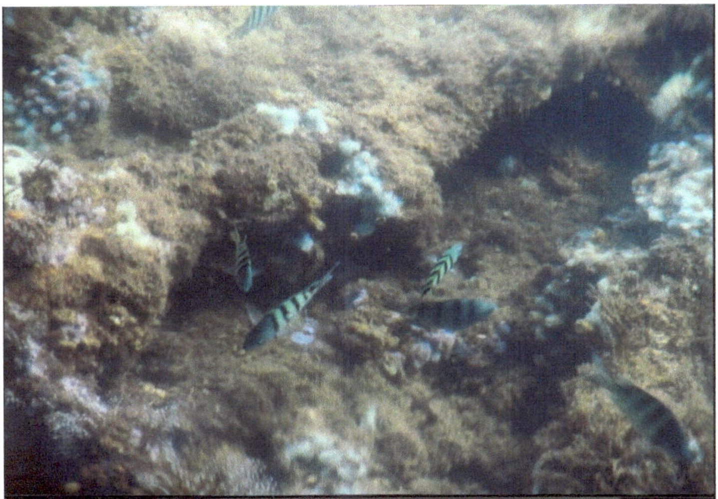

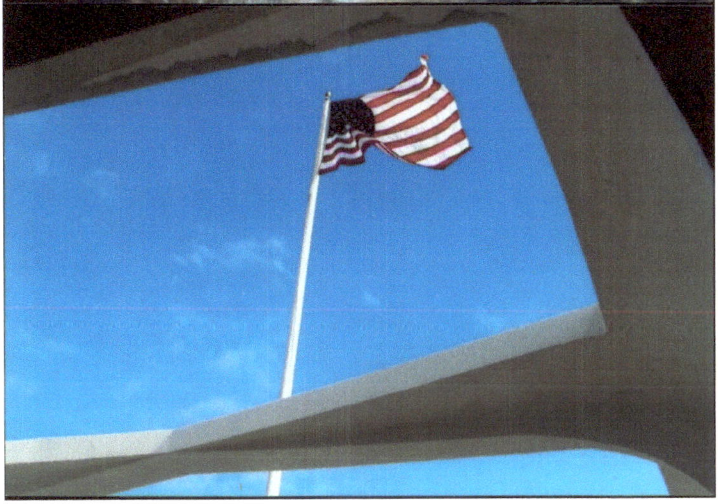

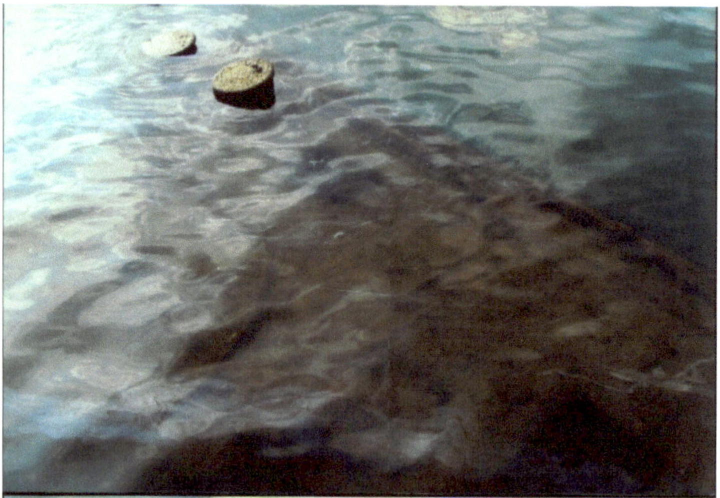

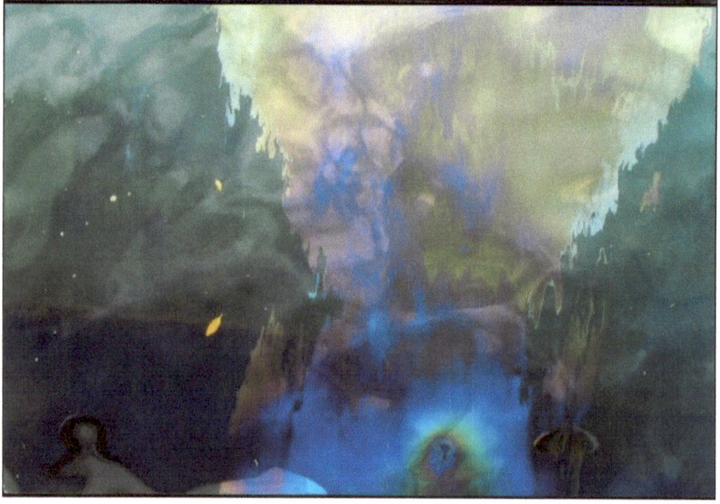

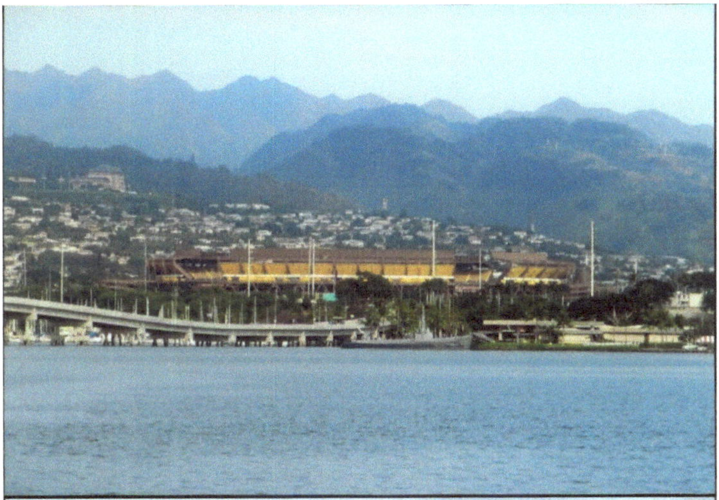

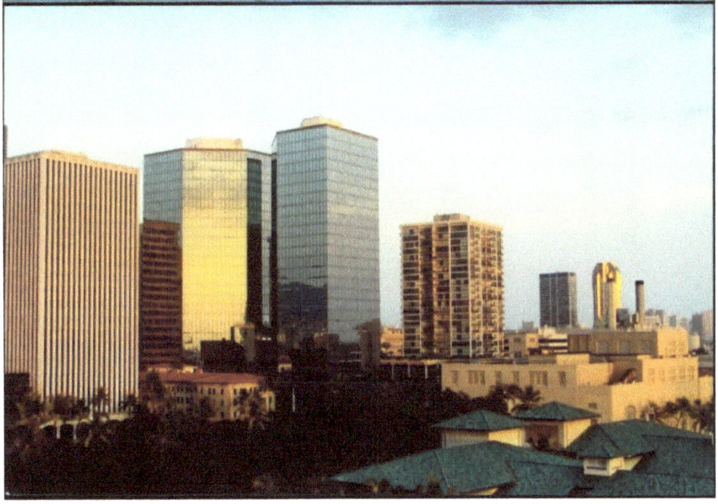

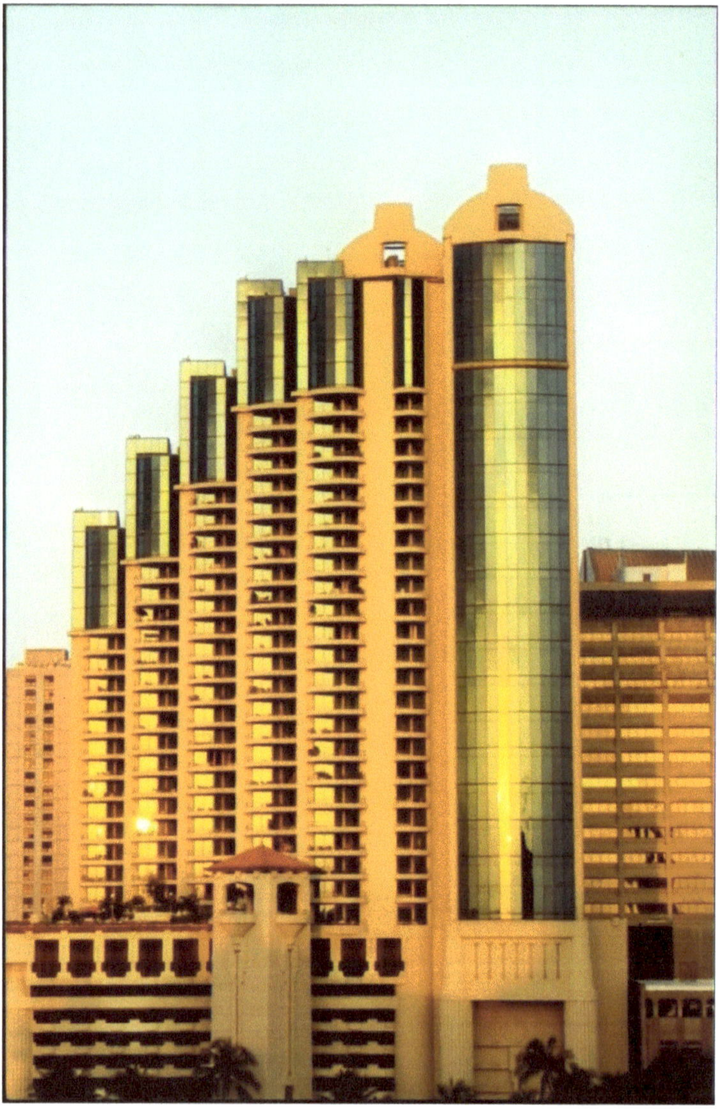

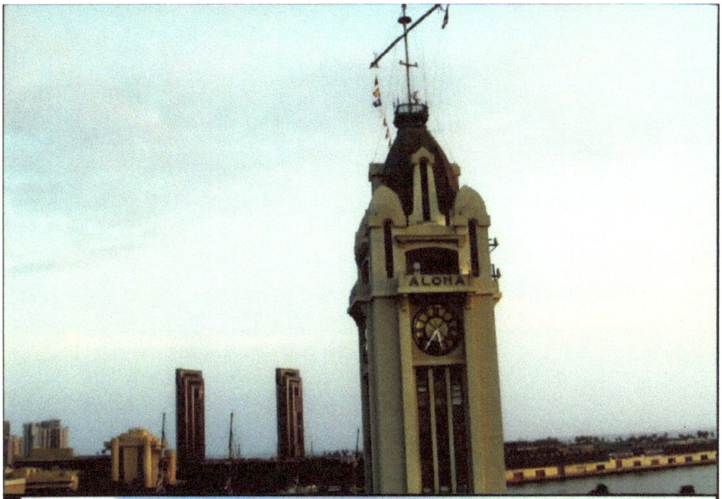
ALOHA

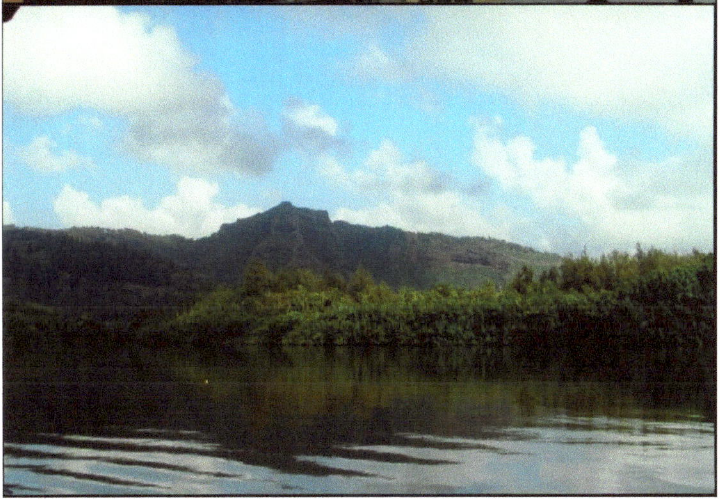

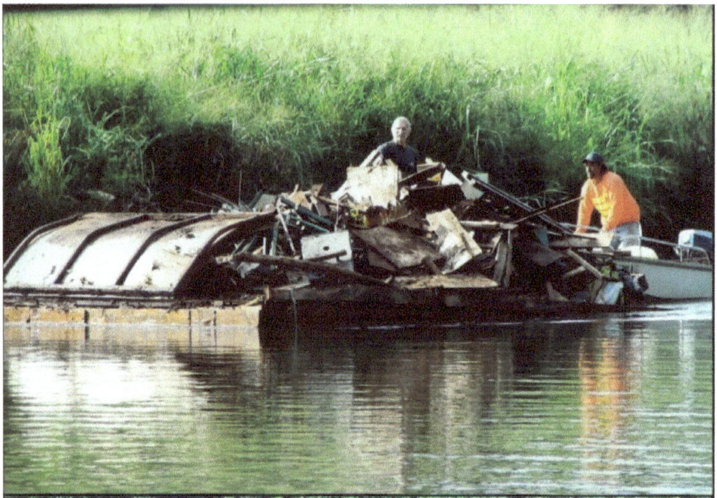

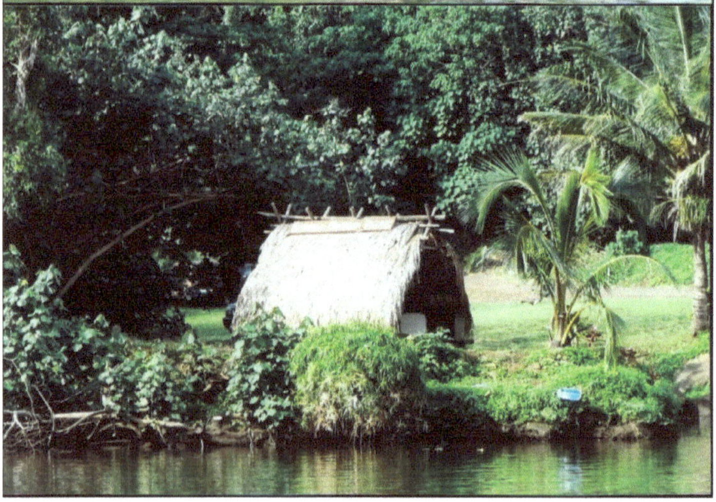

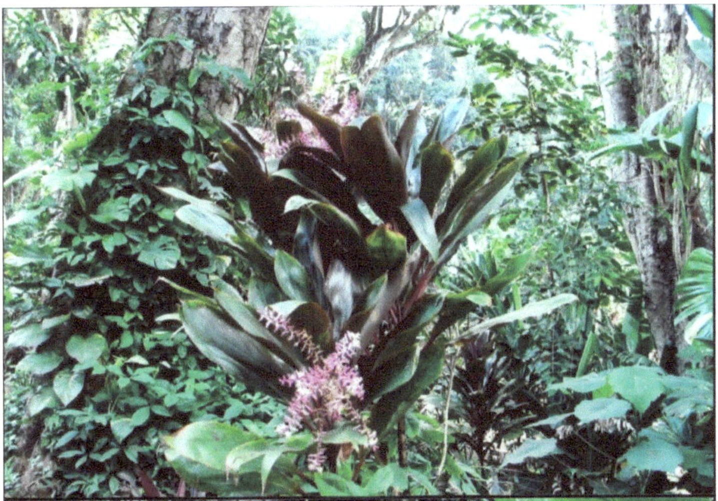

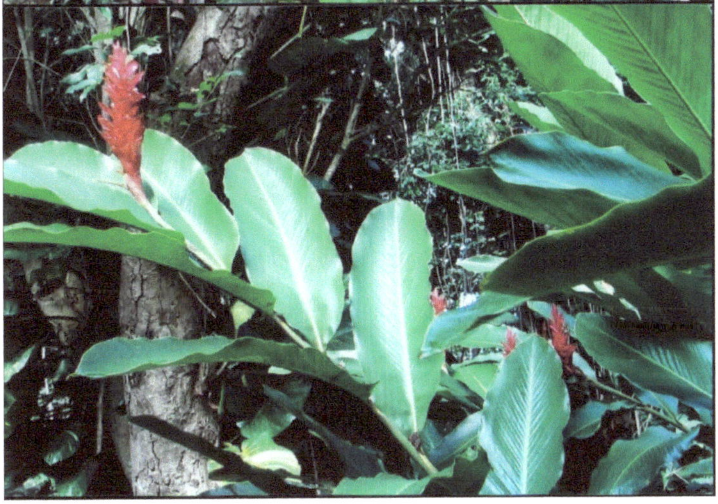

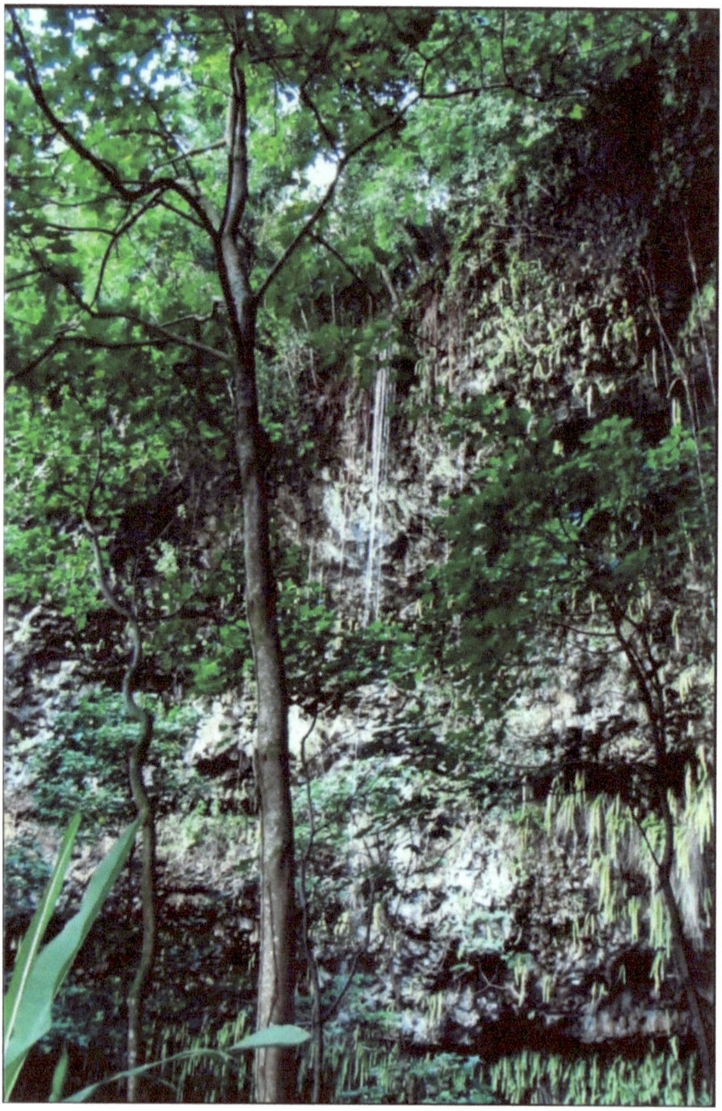

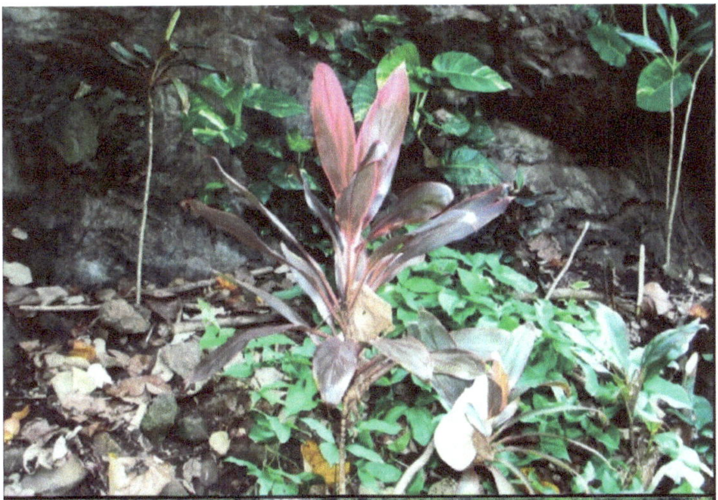

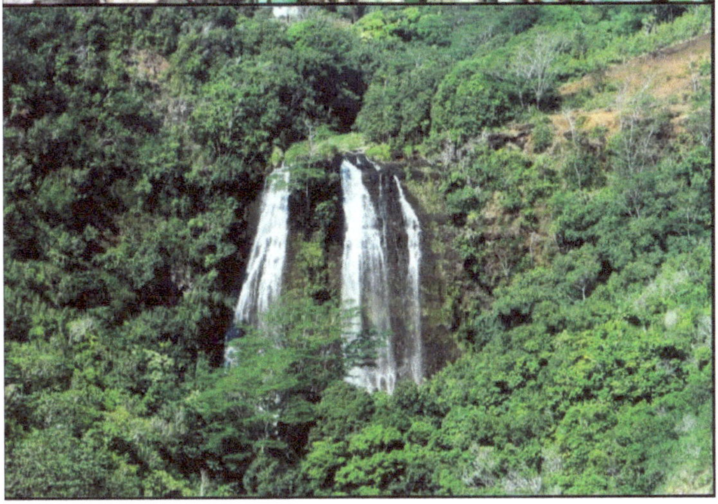

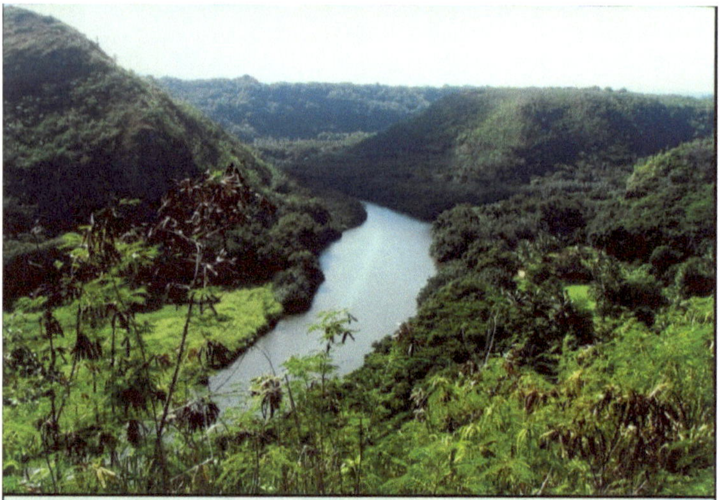

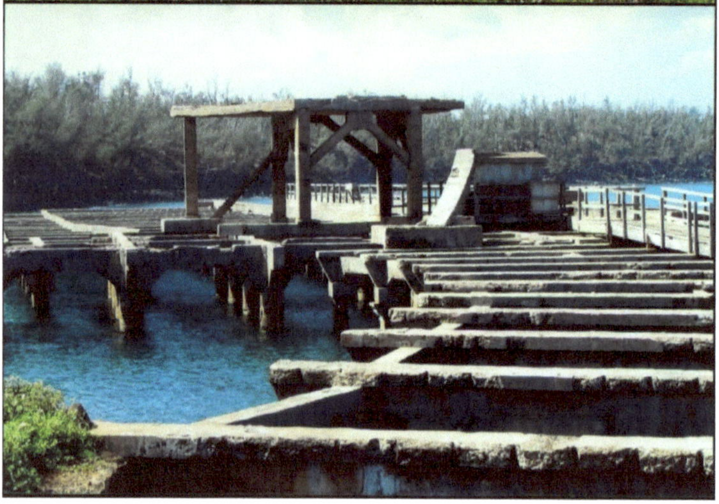

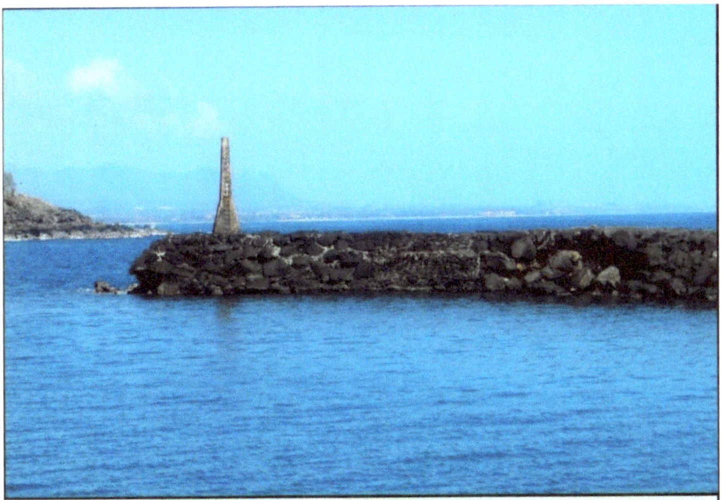
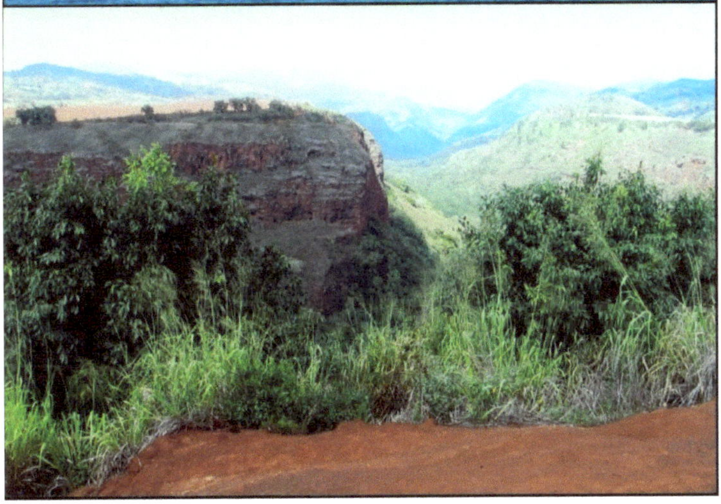

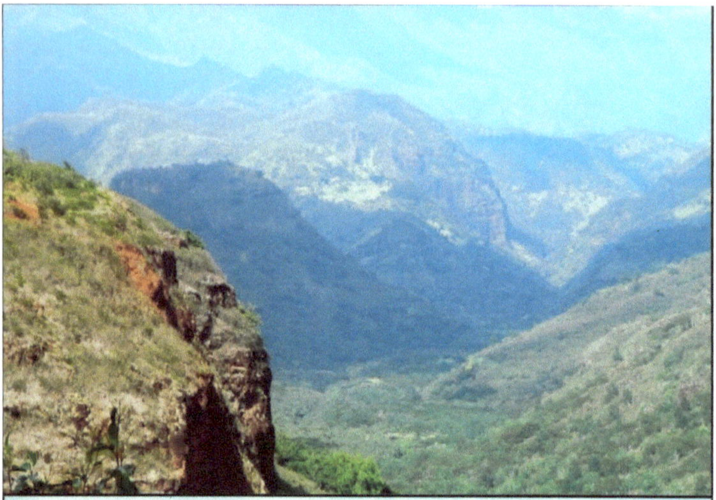
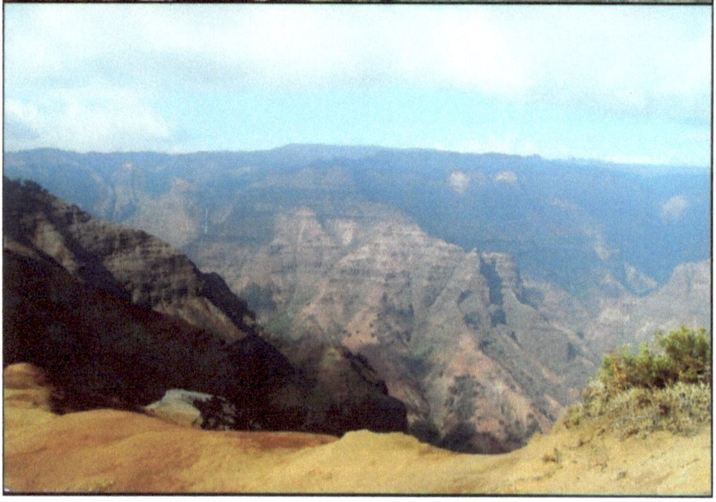

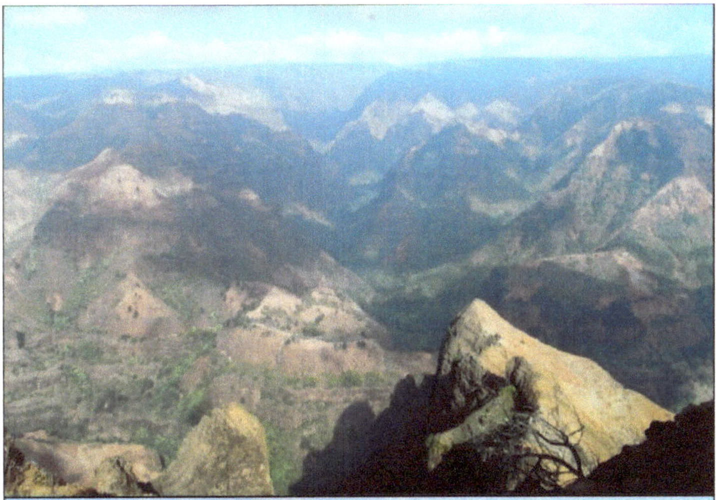
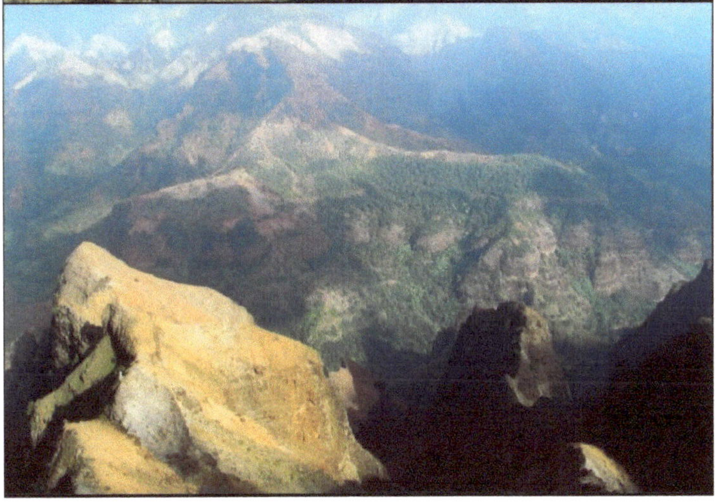

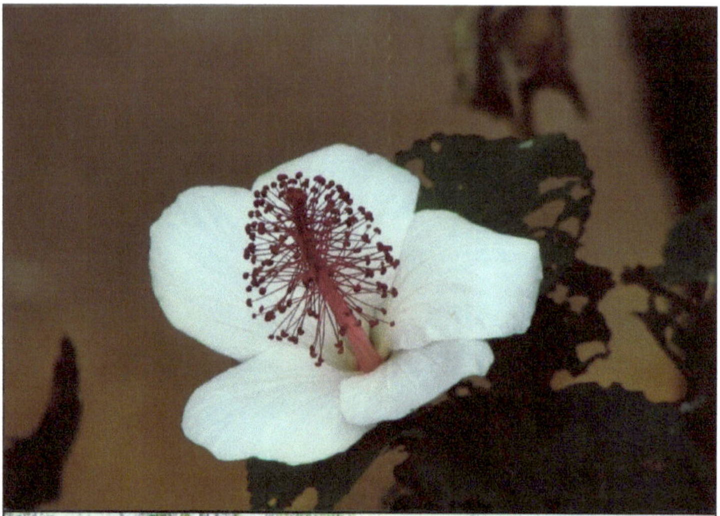
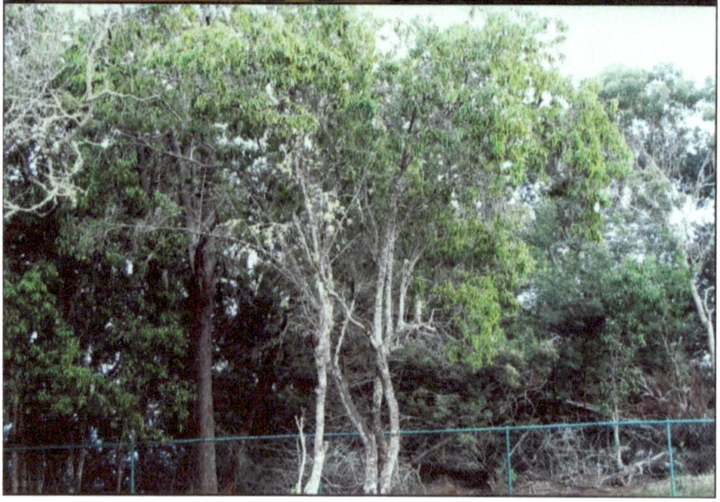

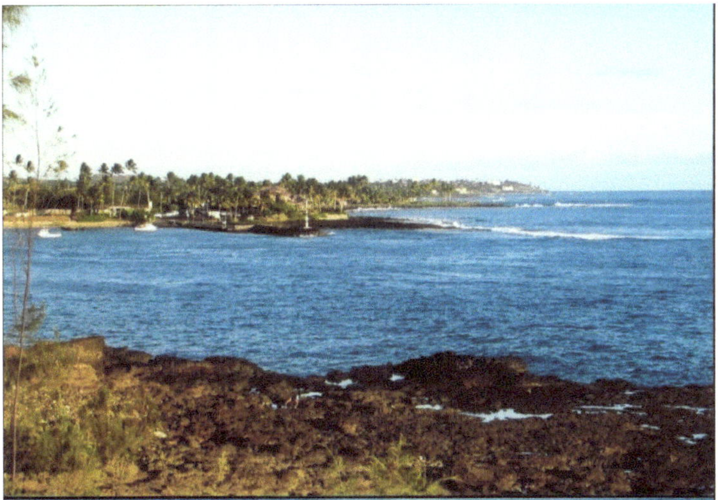

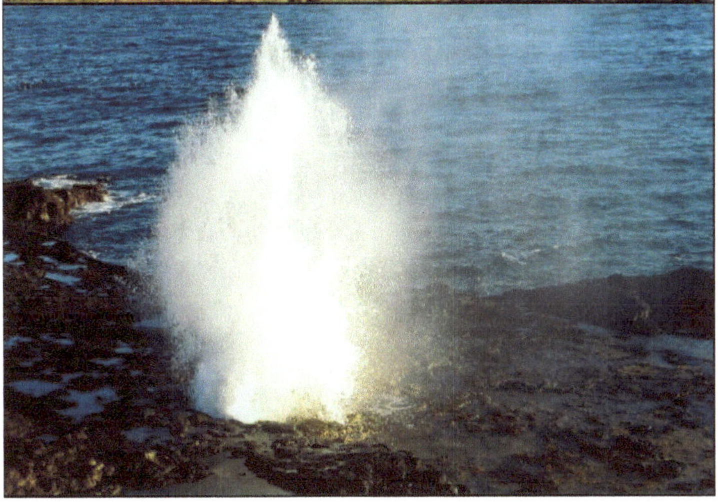

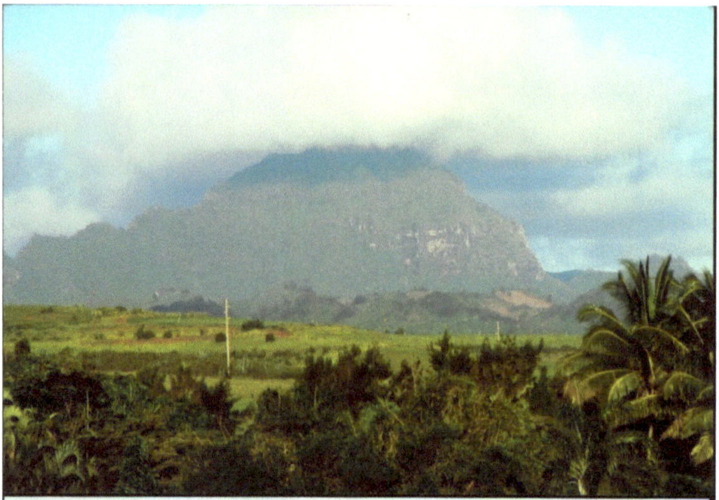
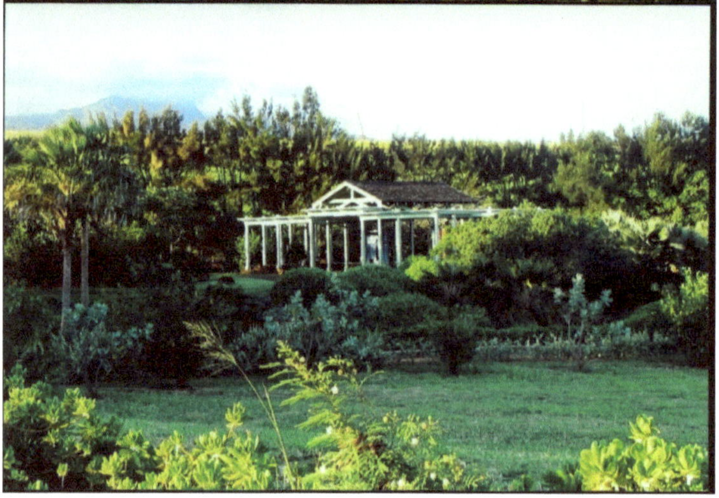

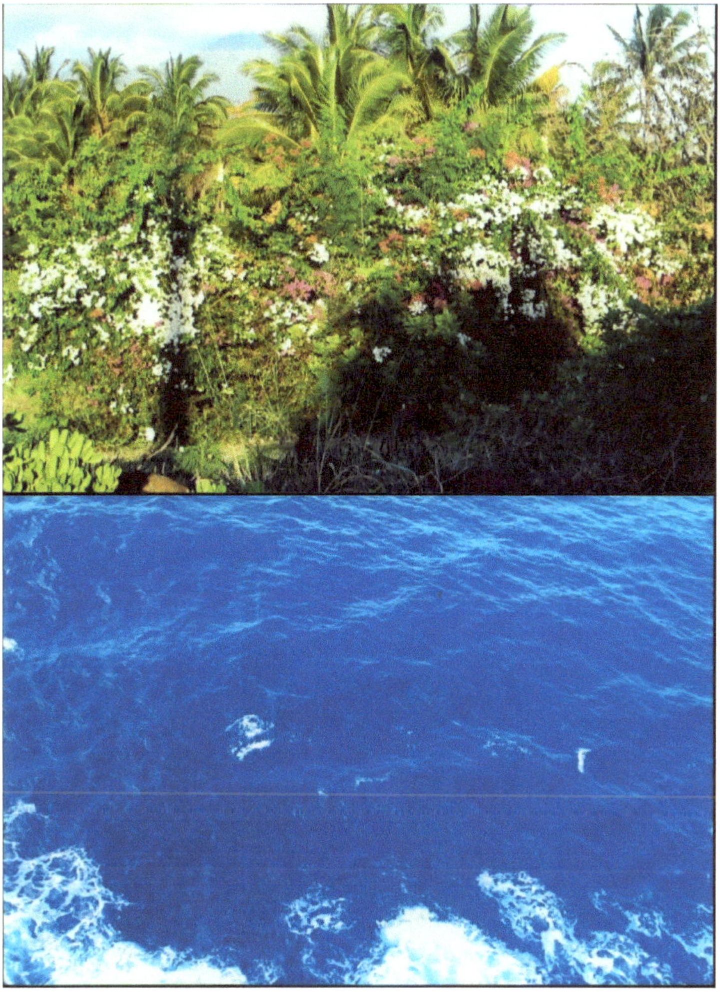

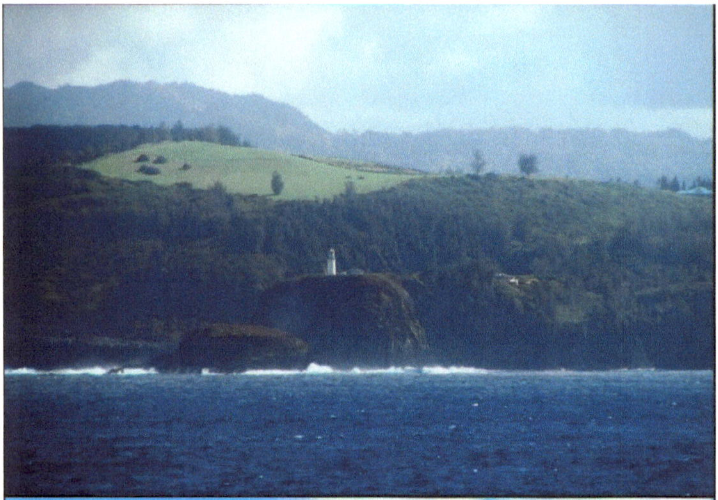

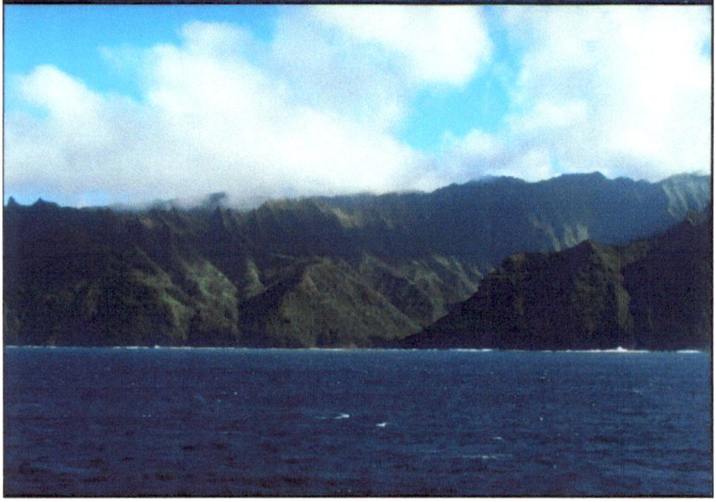

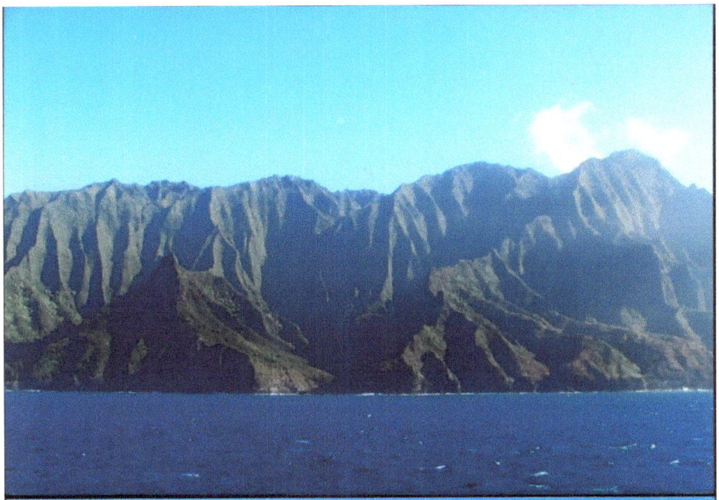

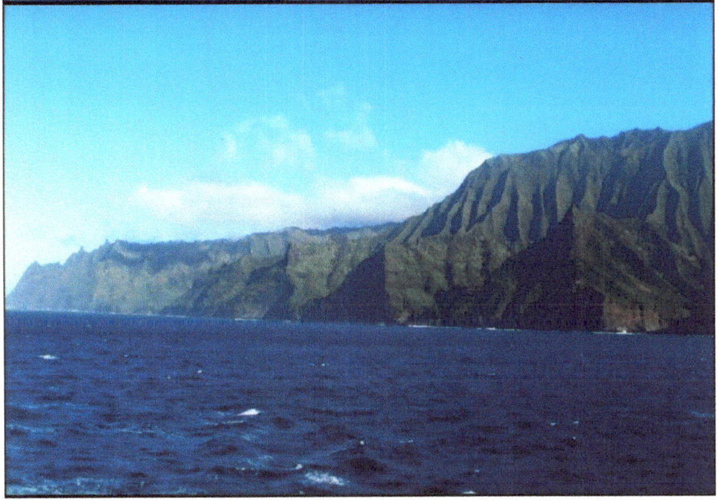

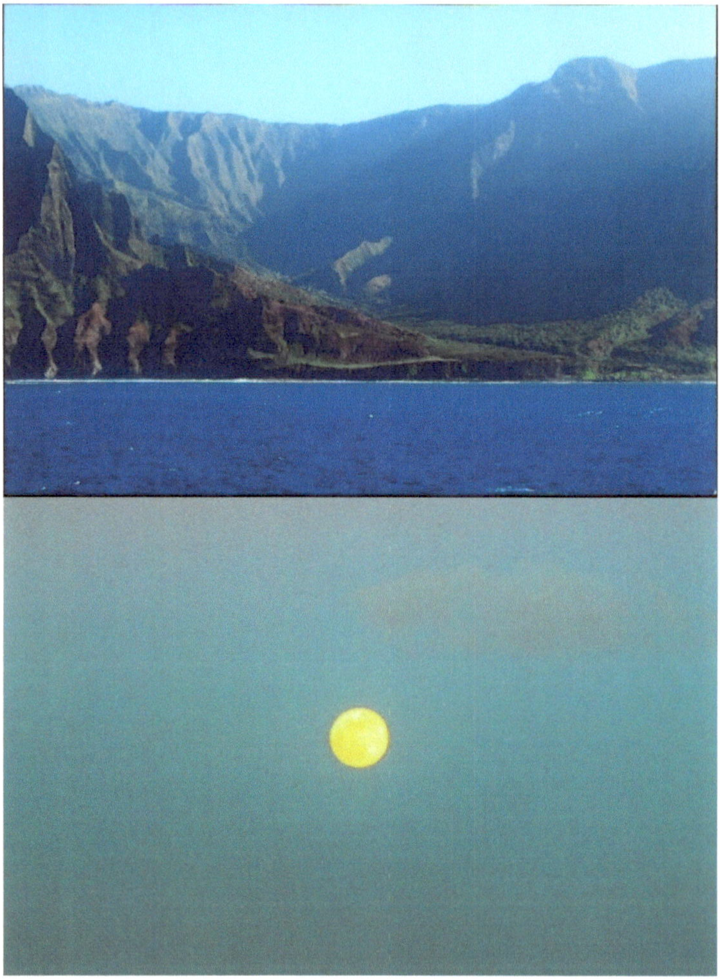

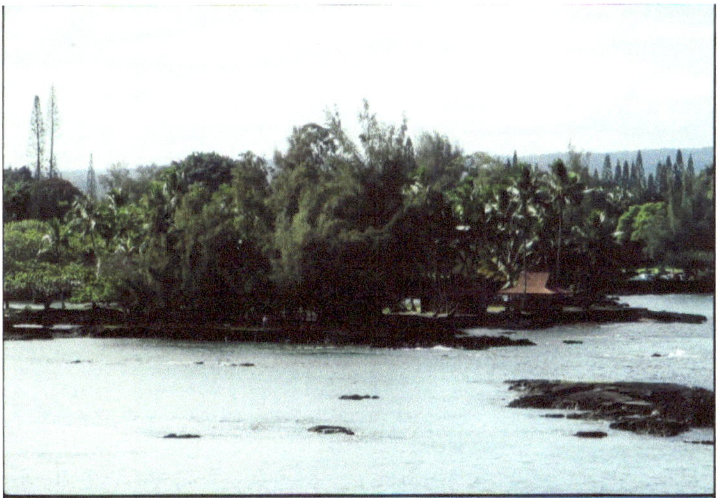

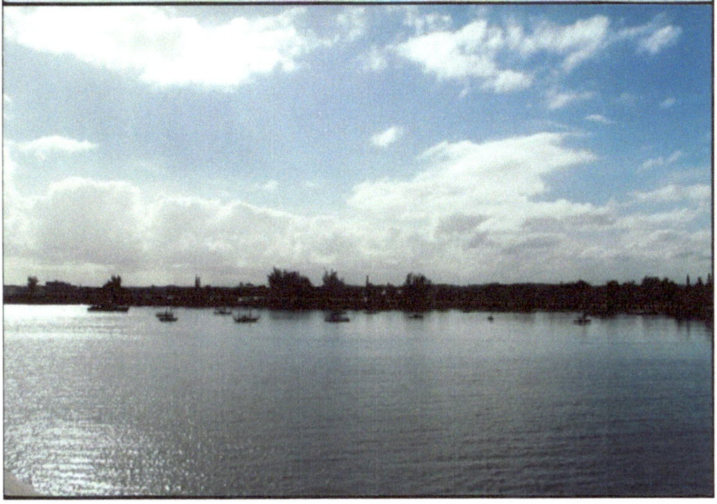

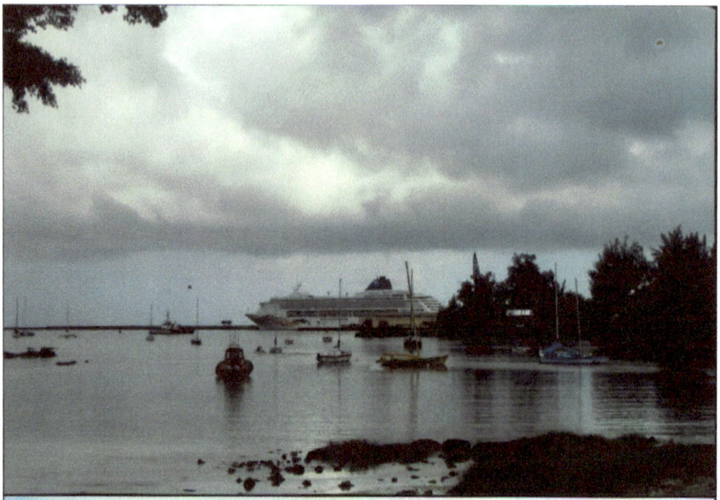

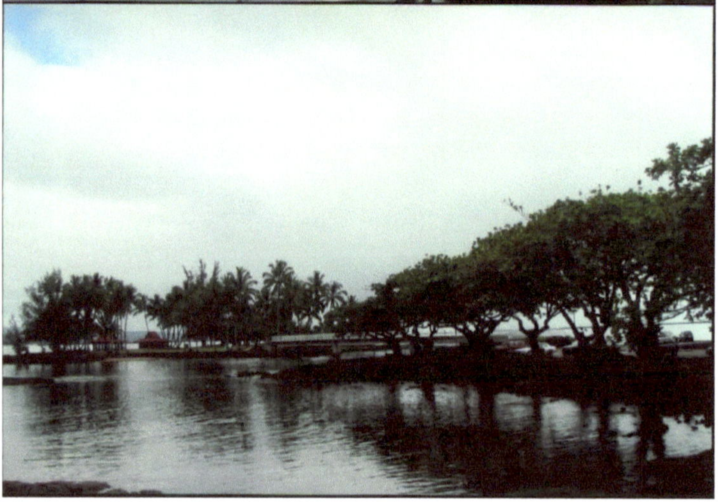

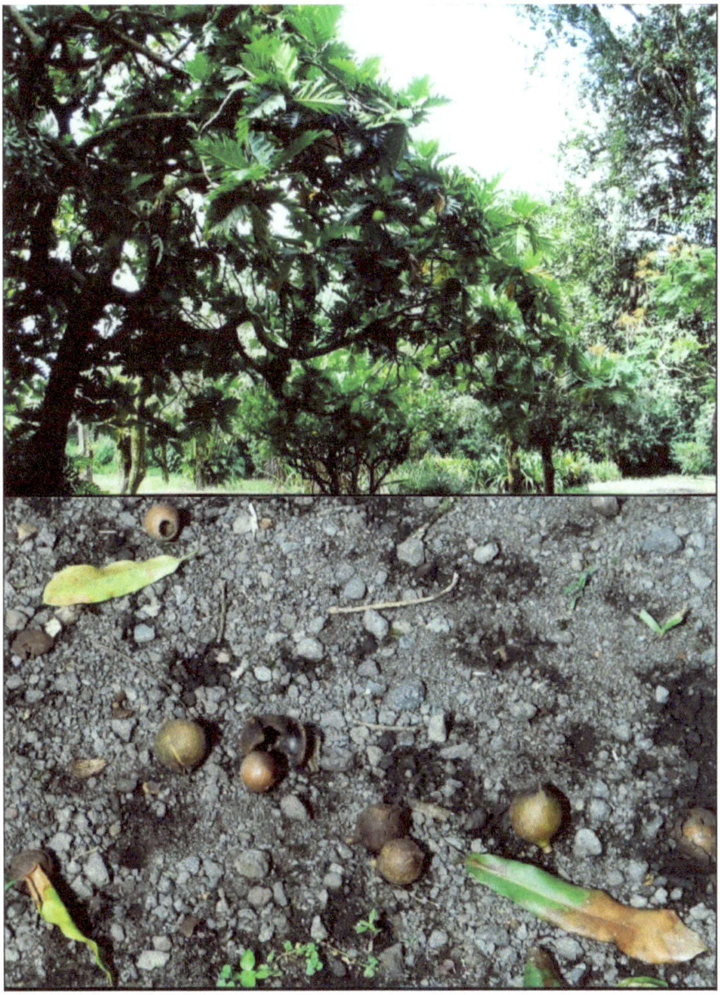

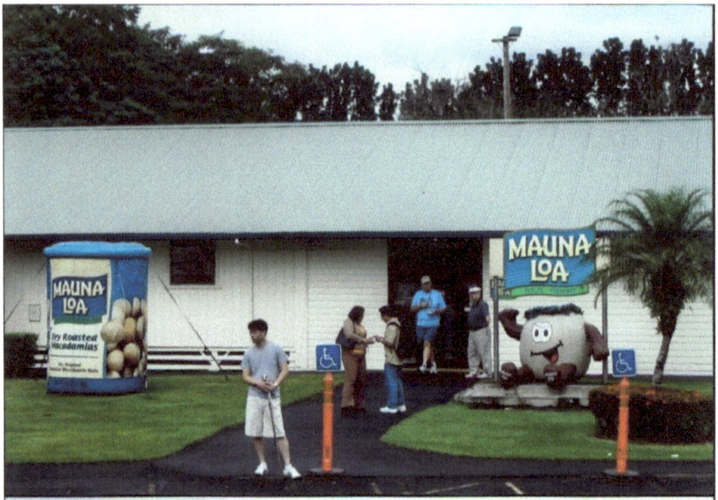
MAUNA LOA
Dry Roasted Macadamias
MAUNA LOA

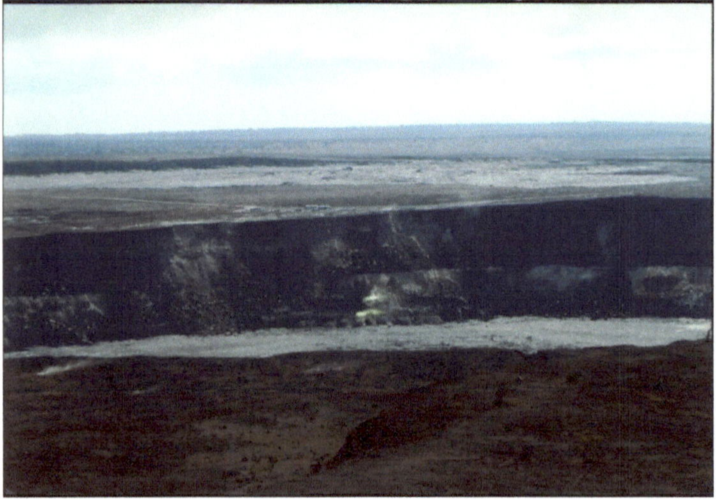

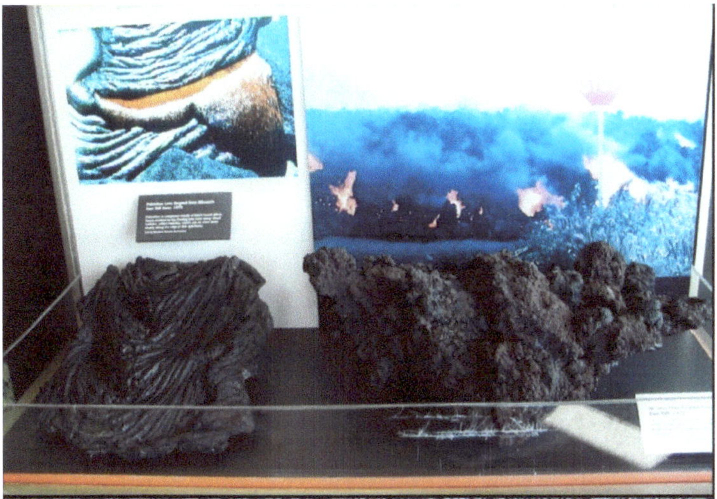

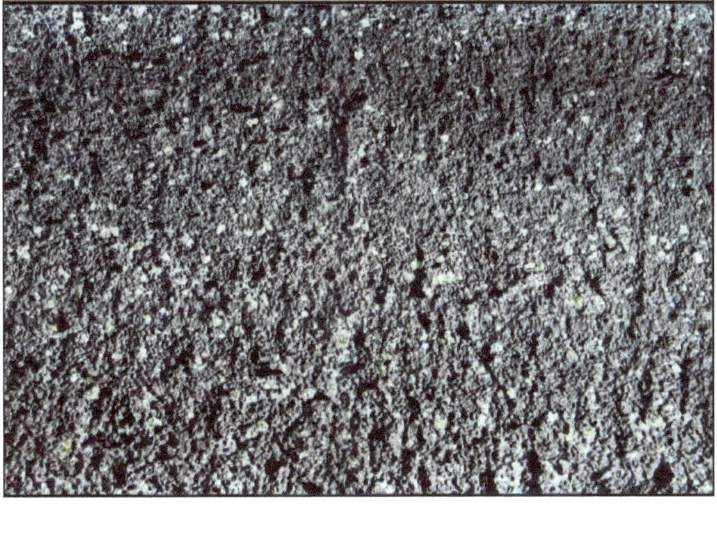

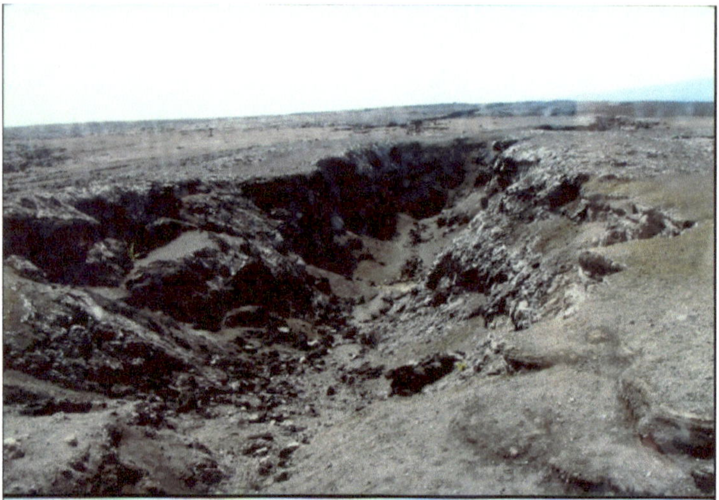

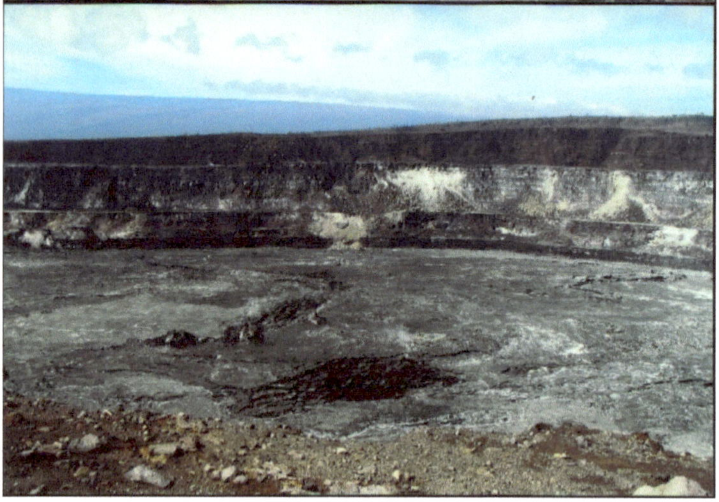

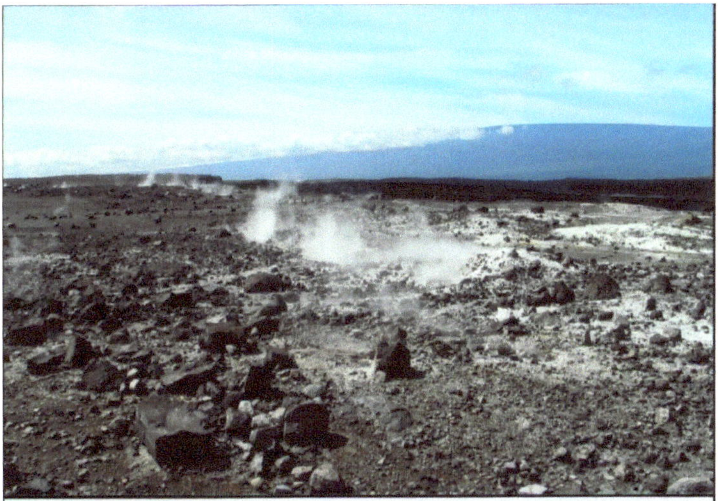

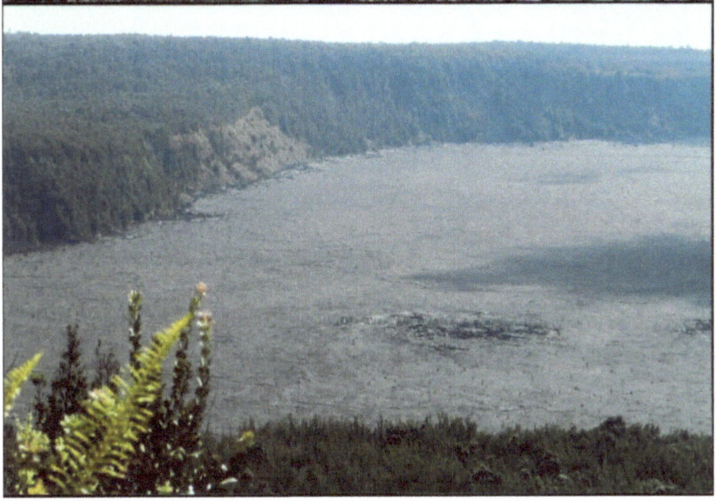

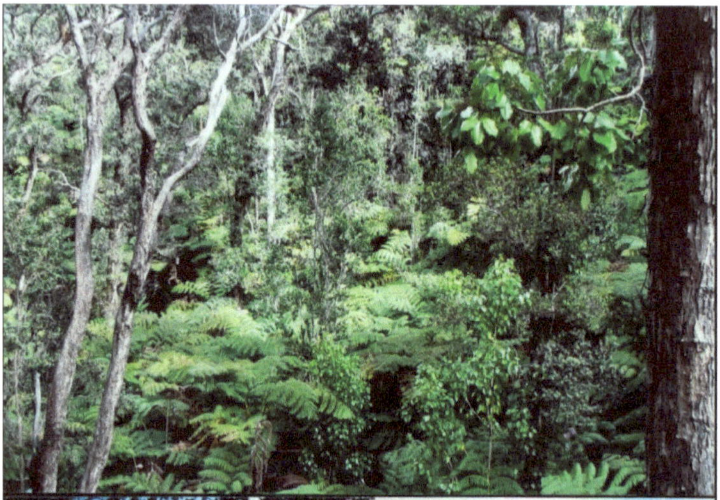

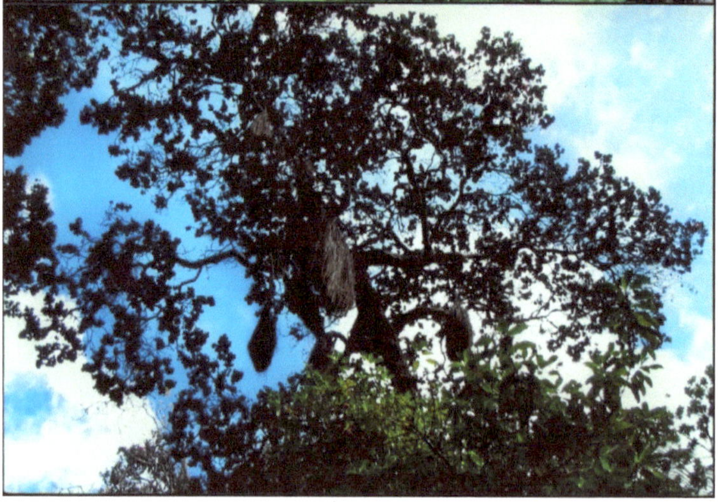

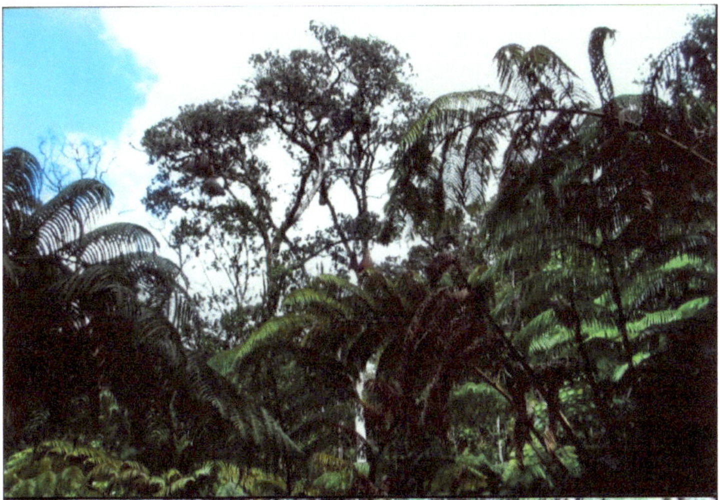
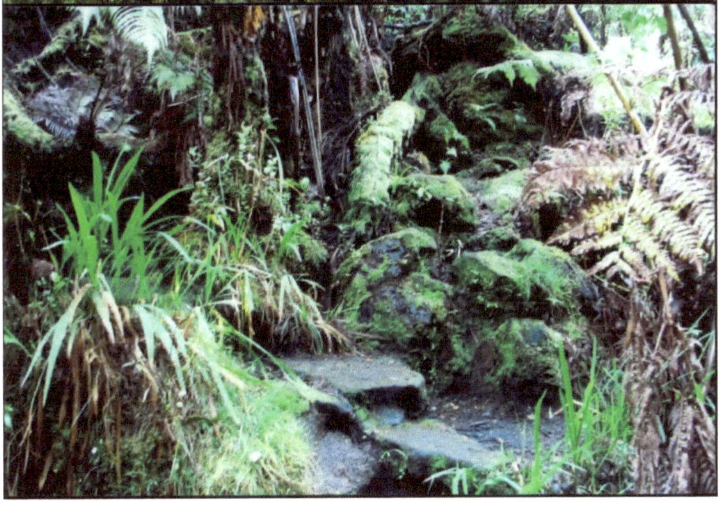

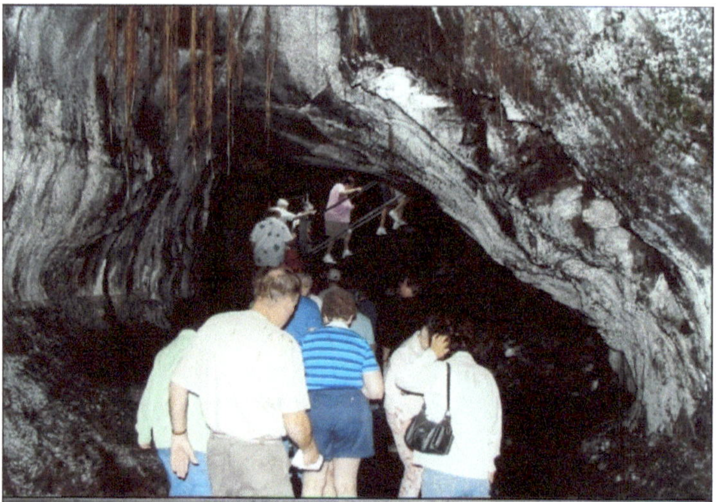
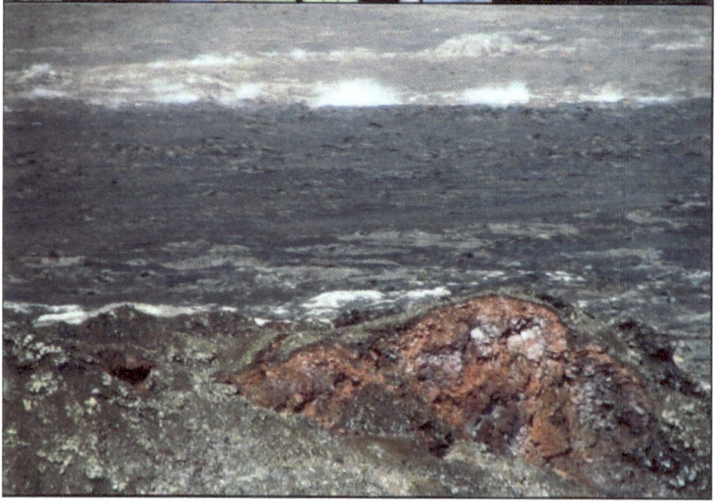

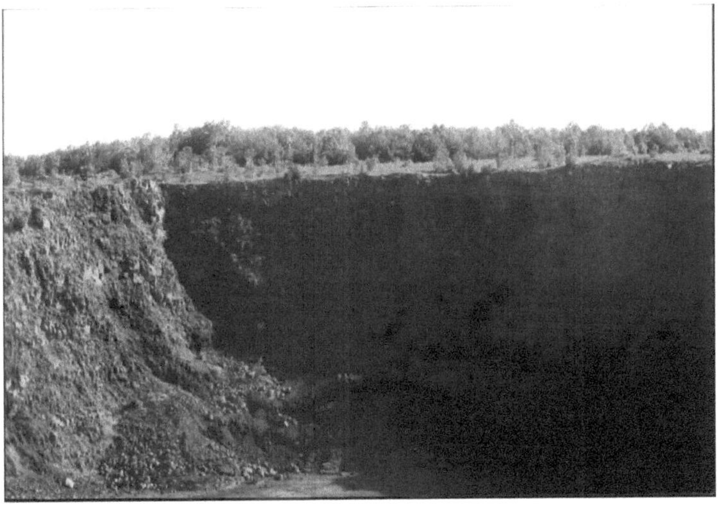

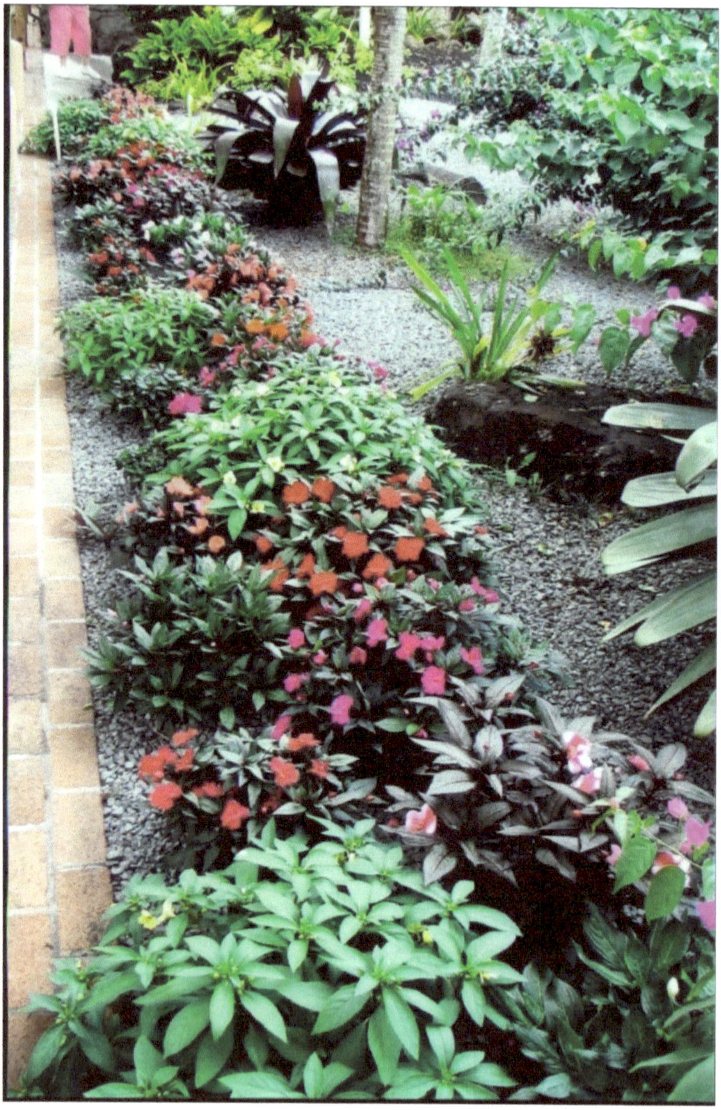

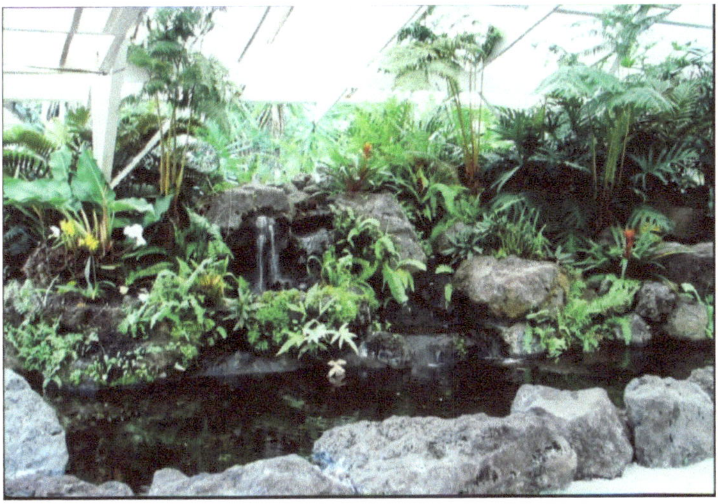

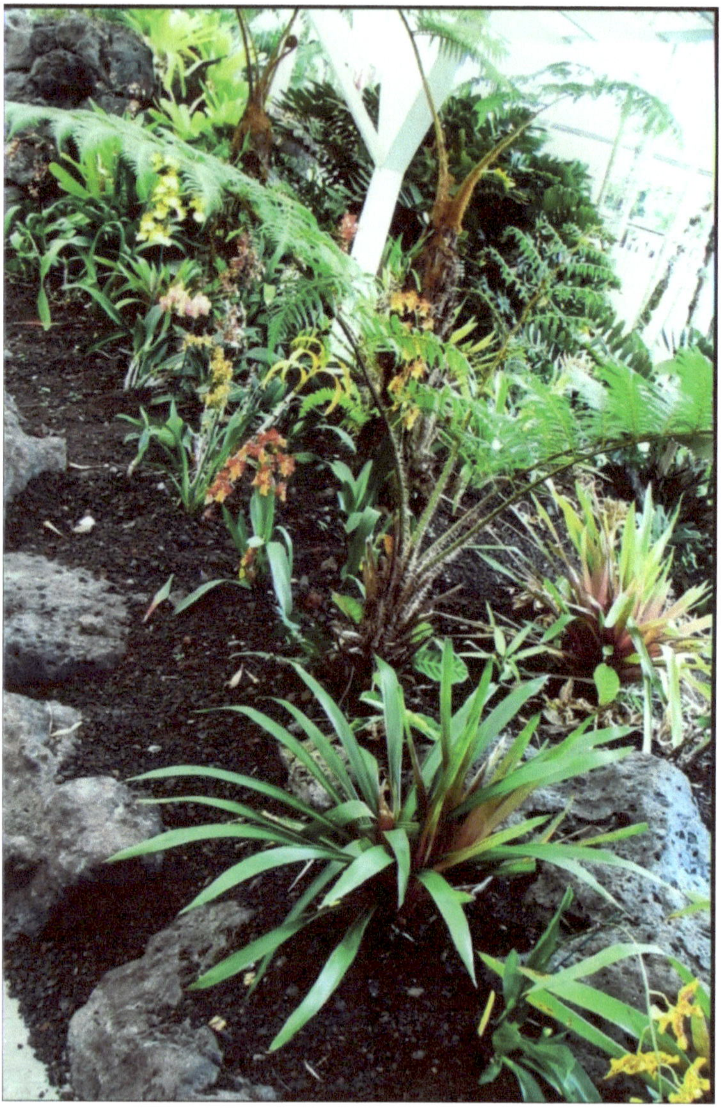

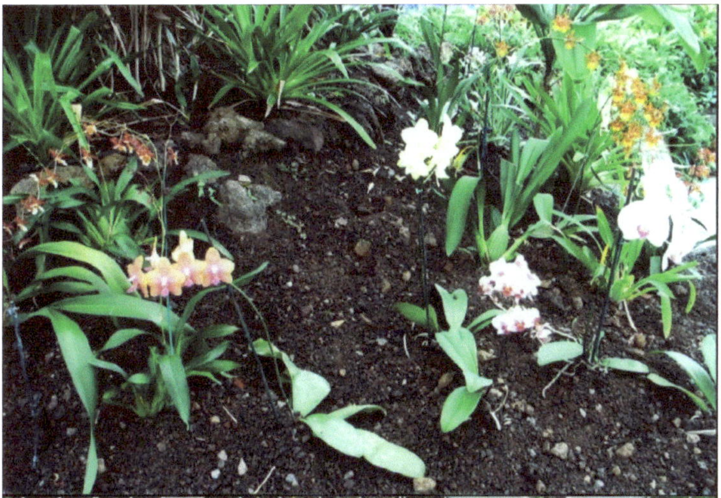

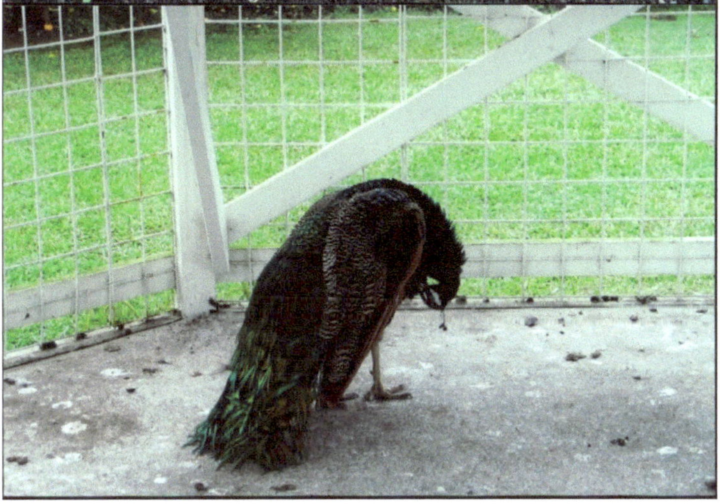

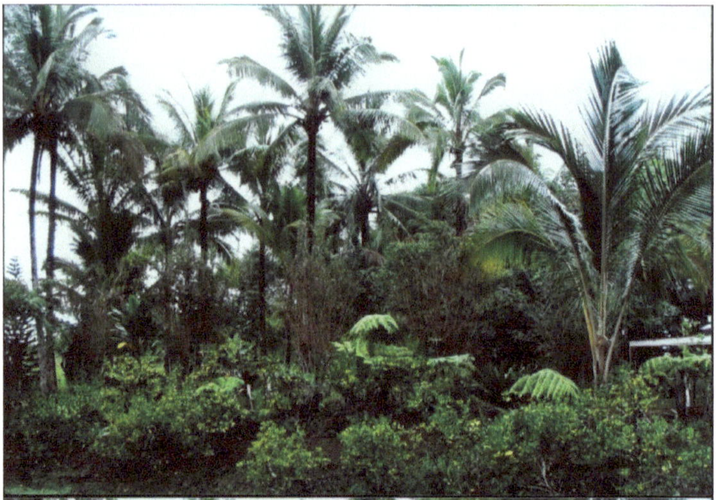

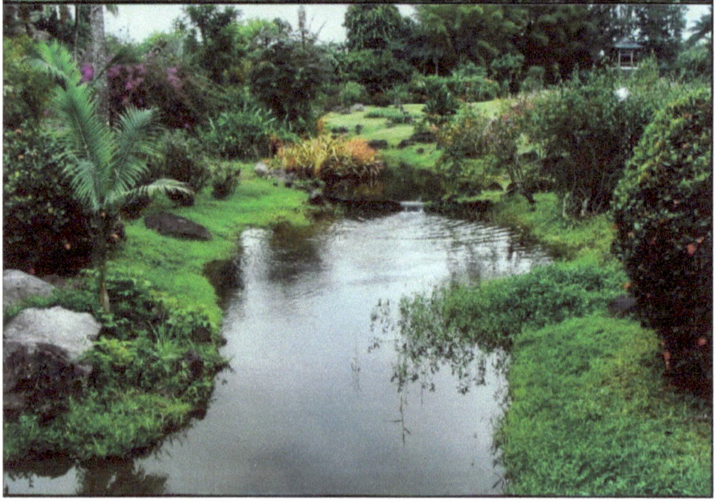

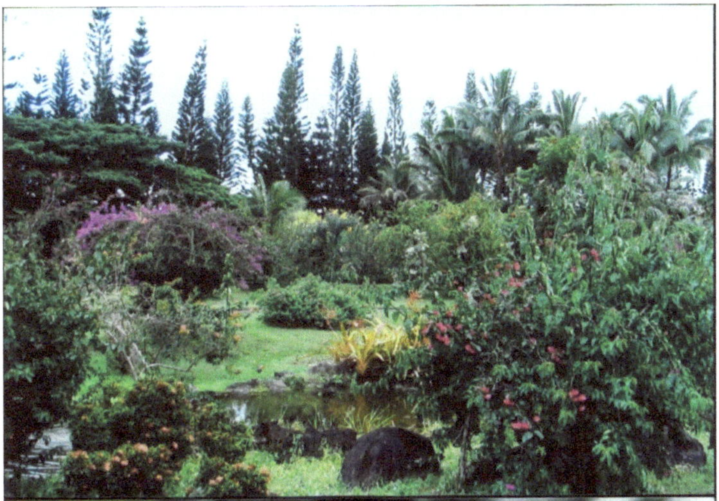

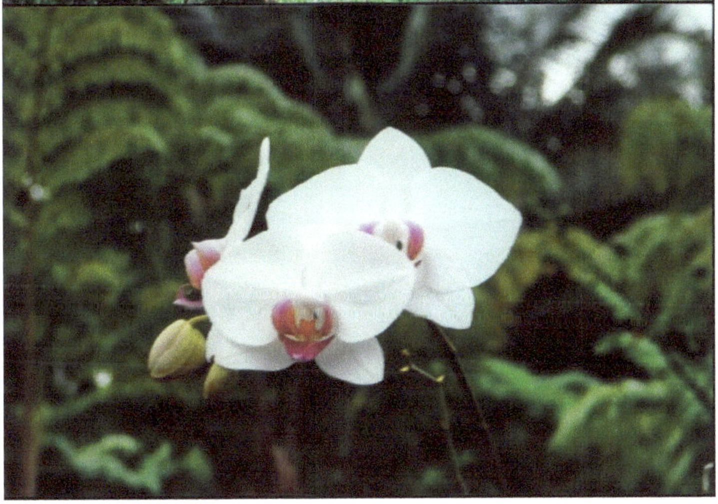

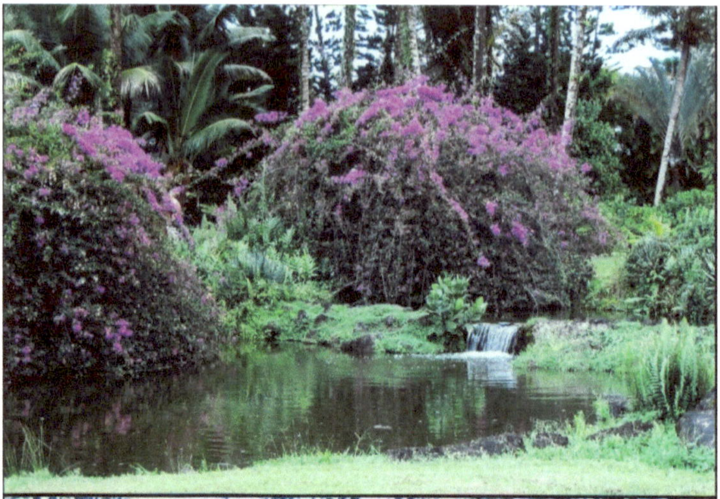

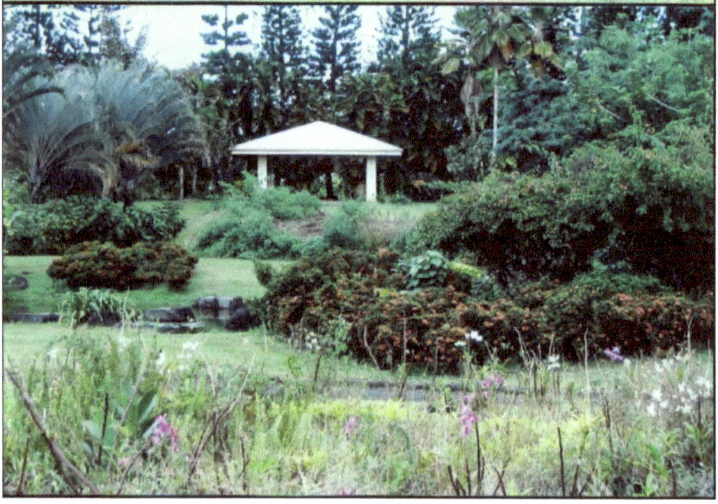

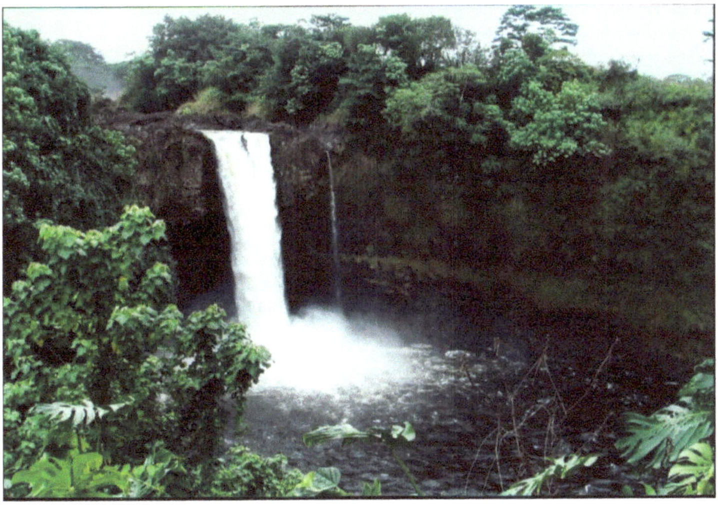

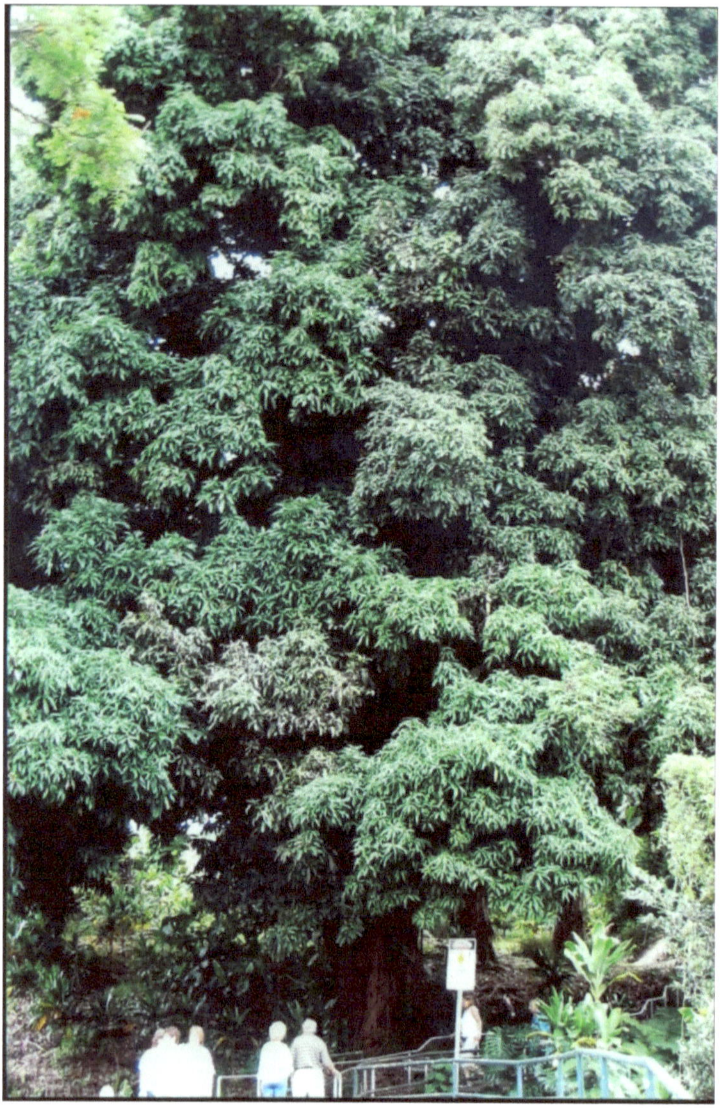

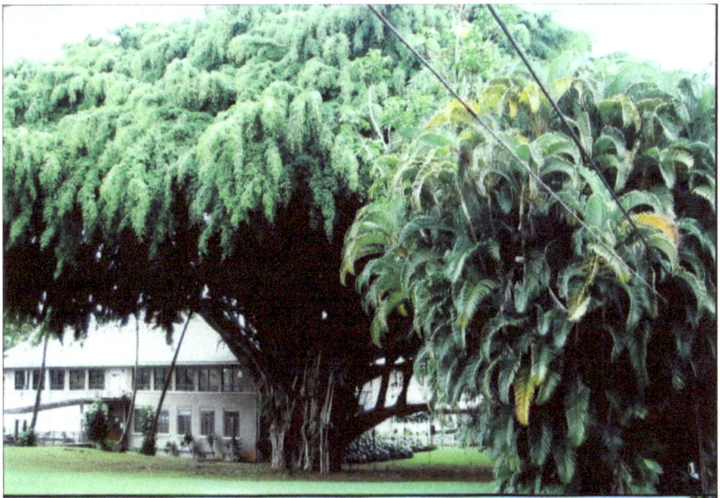
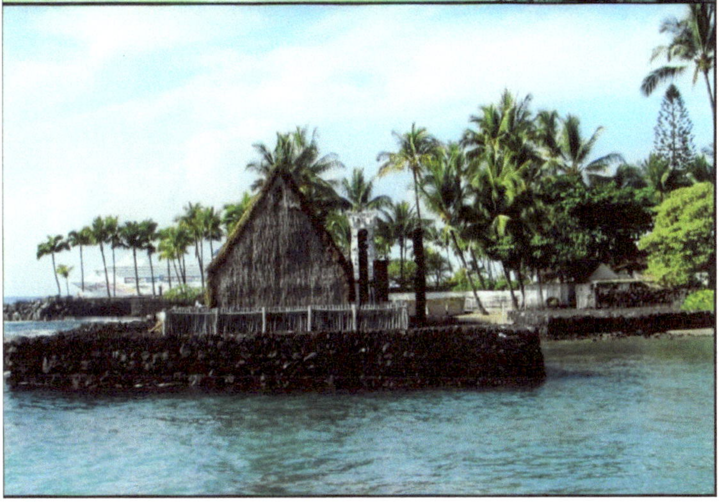

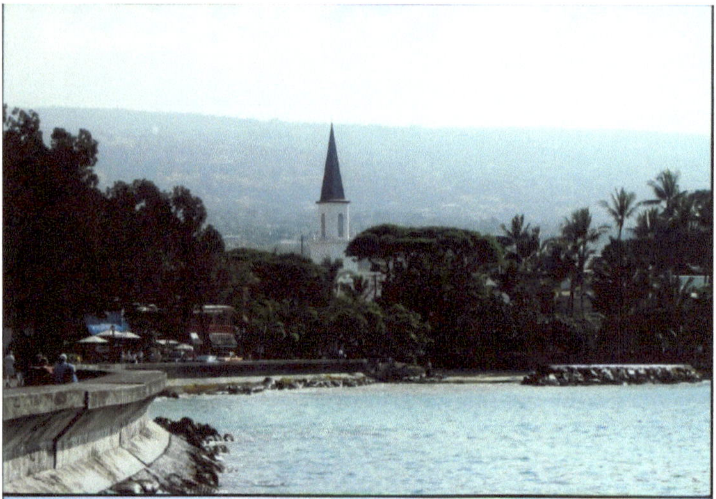

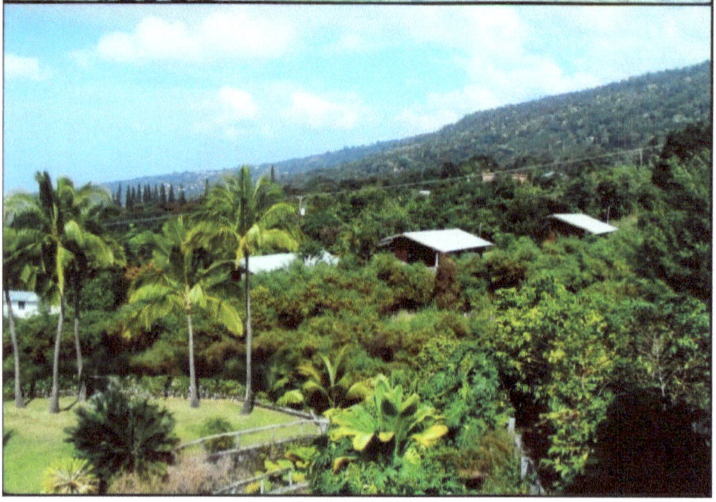

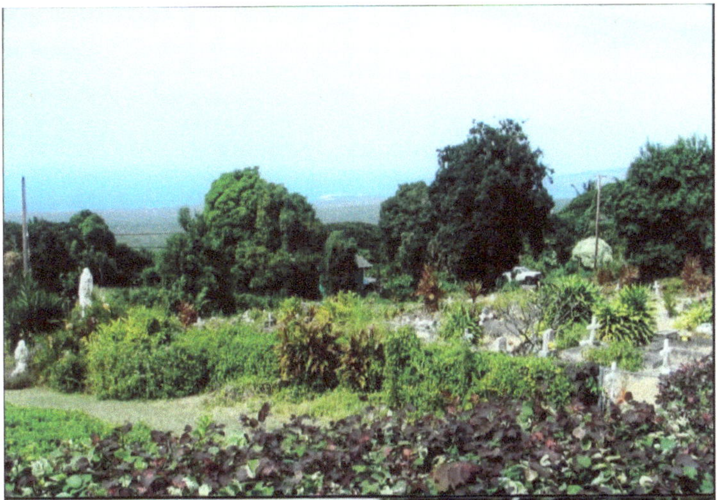
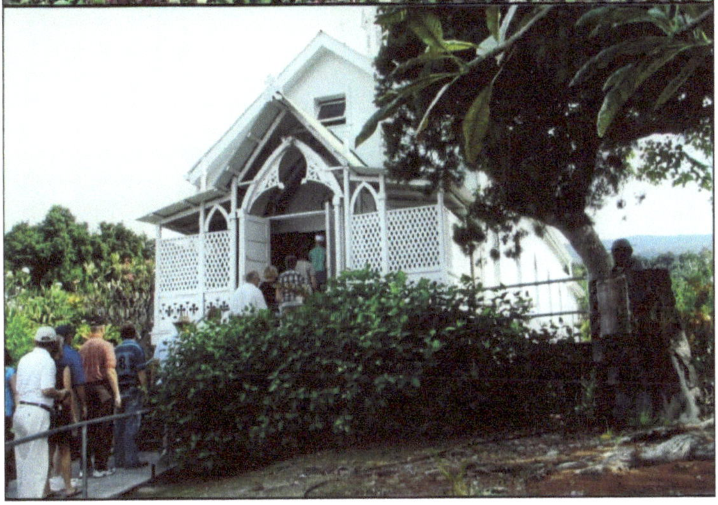

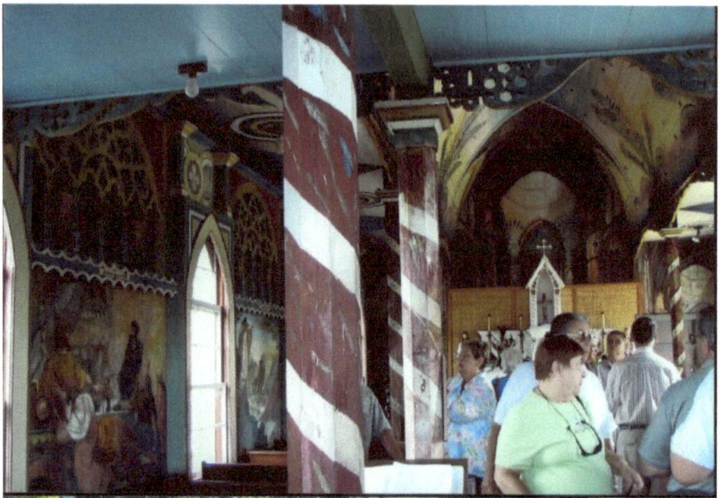
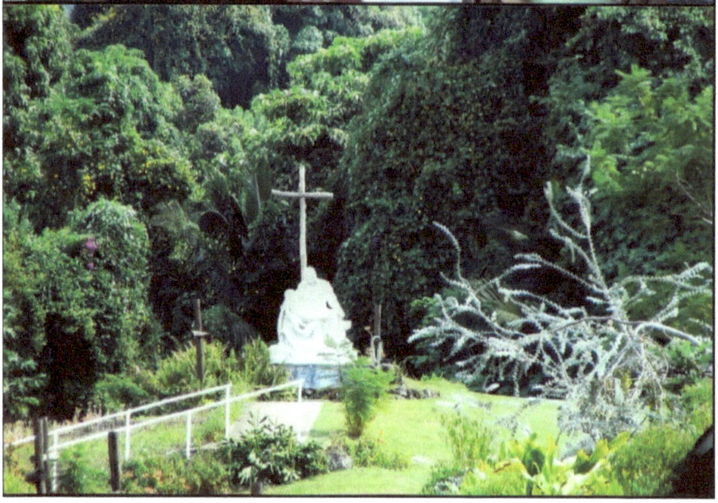

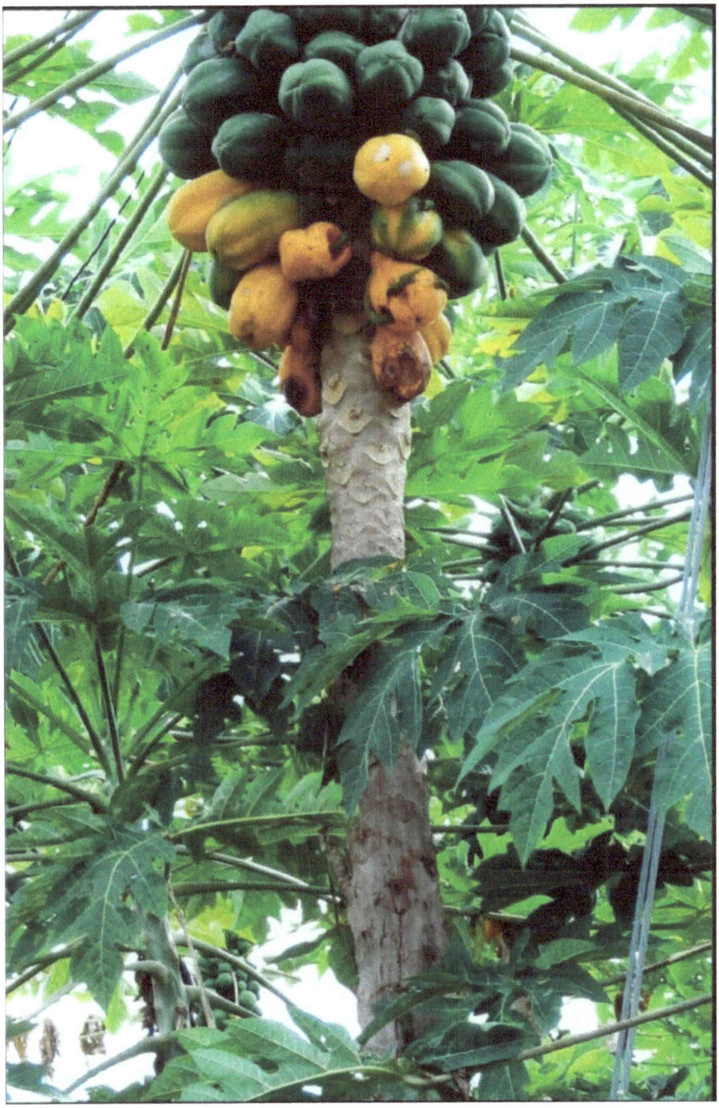

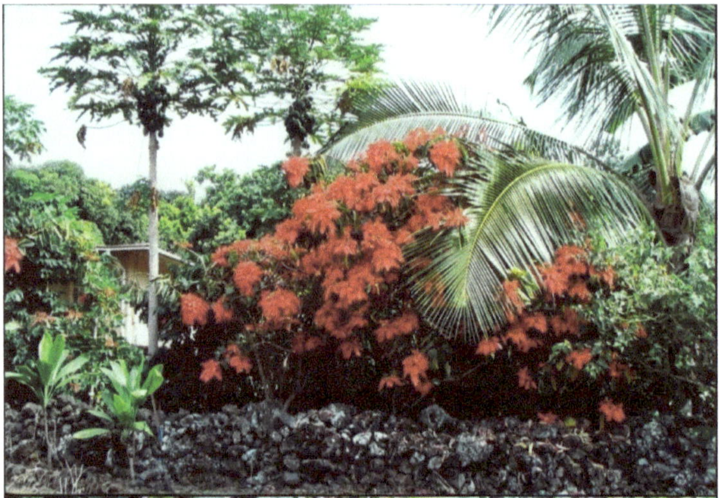

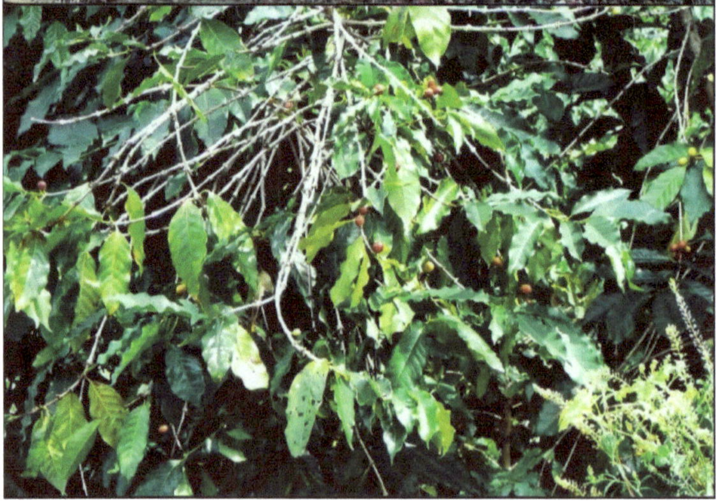

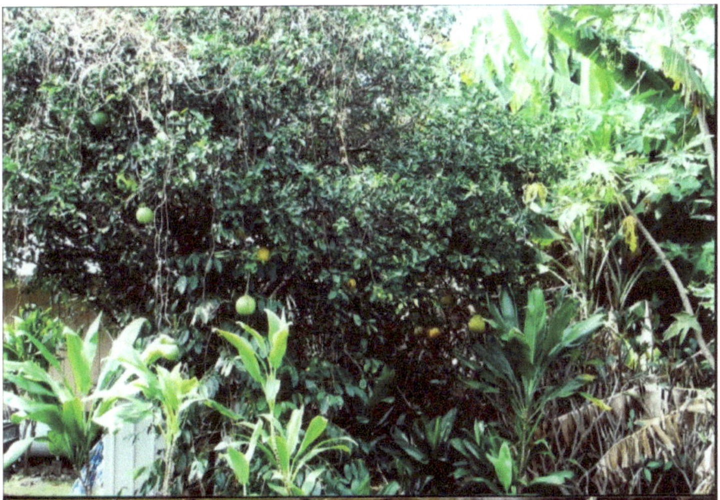

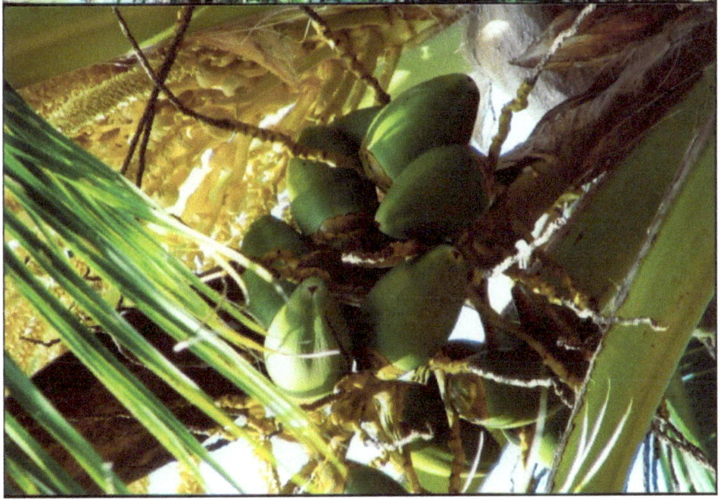

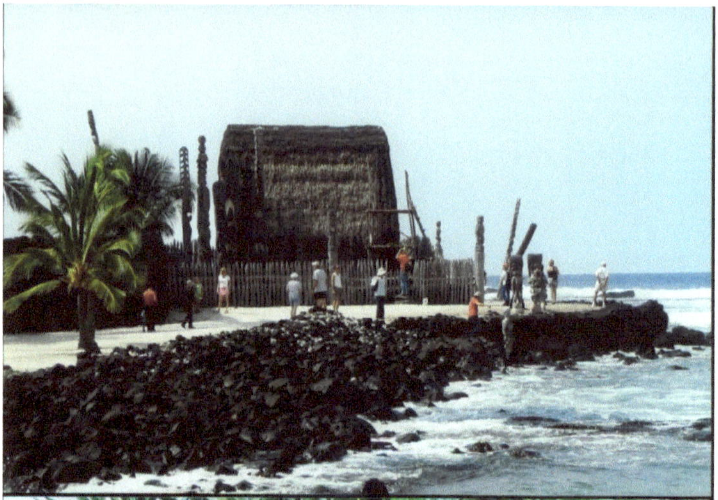

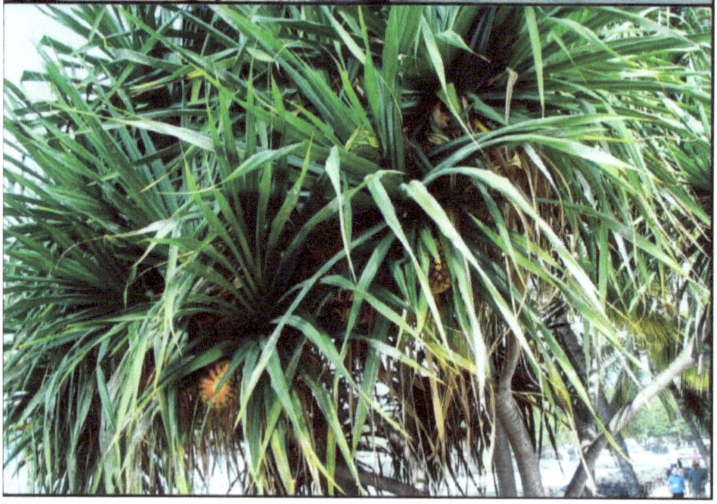

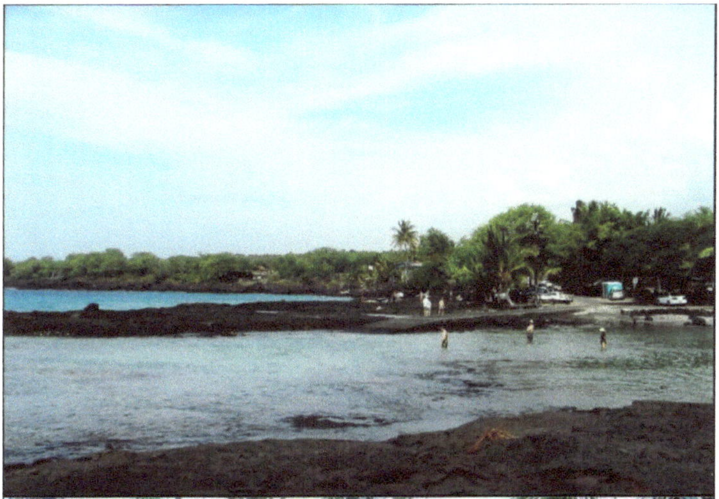

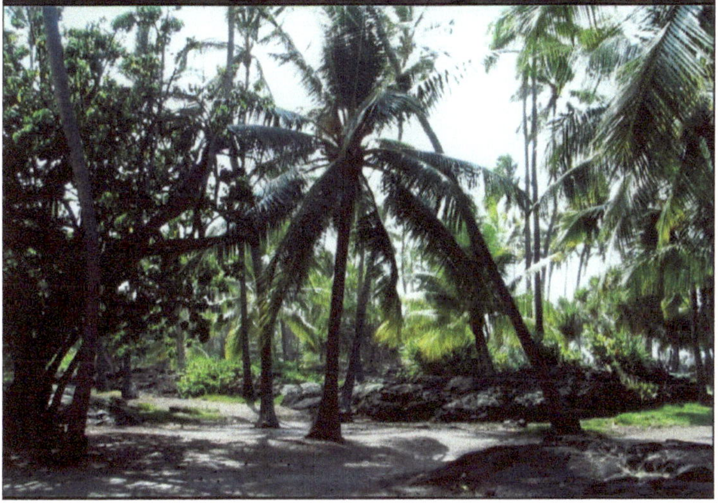

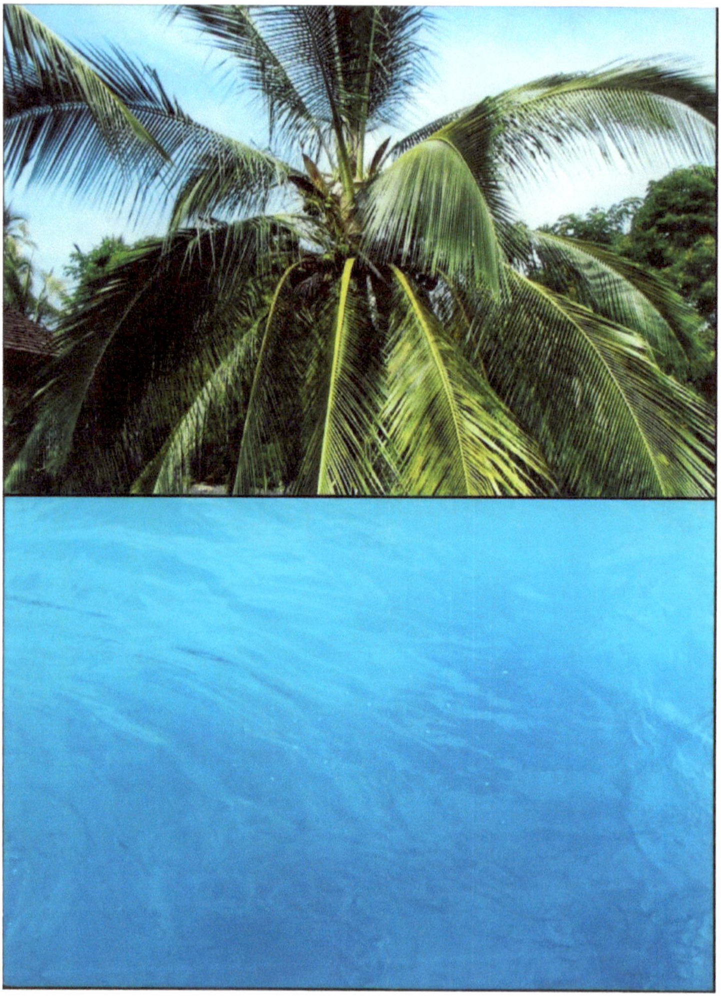

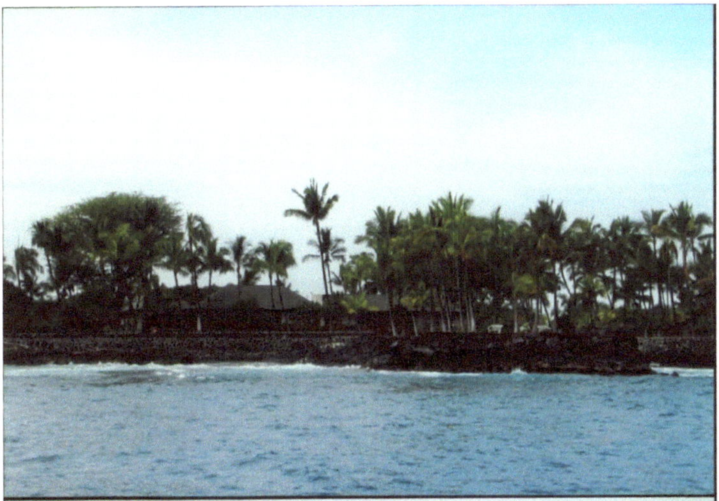

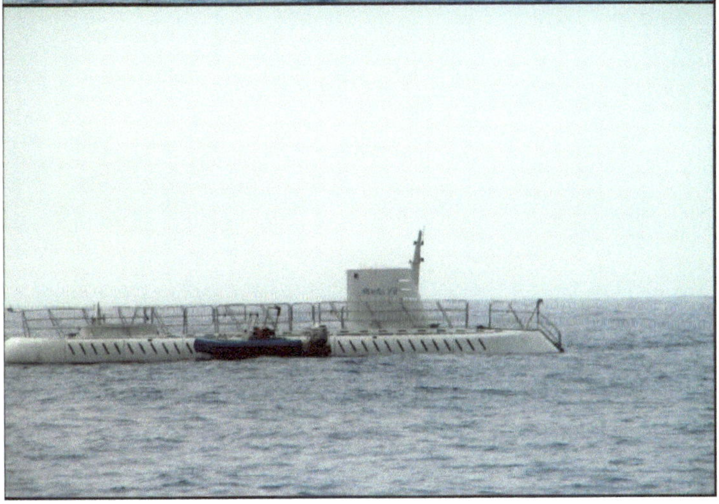

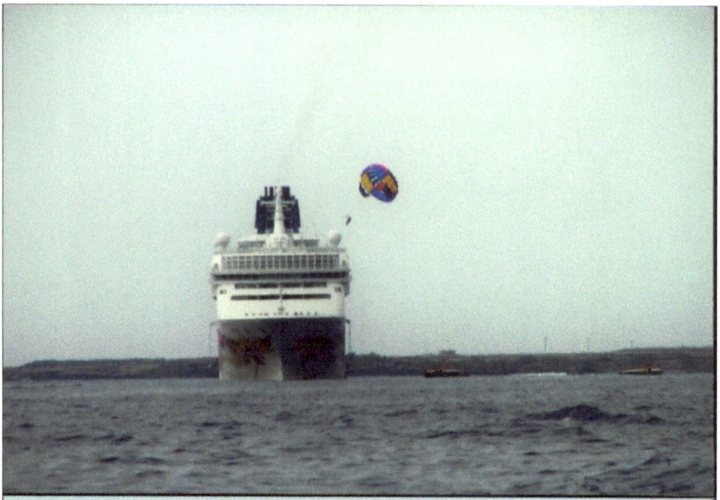

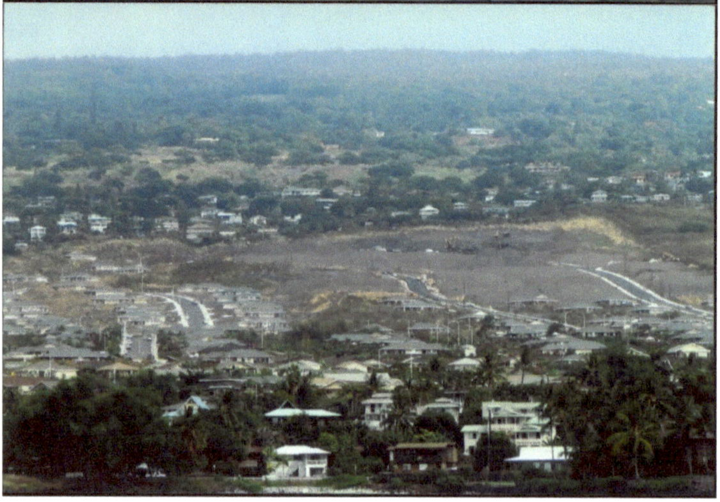

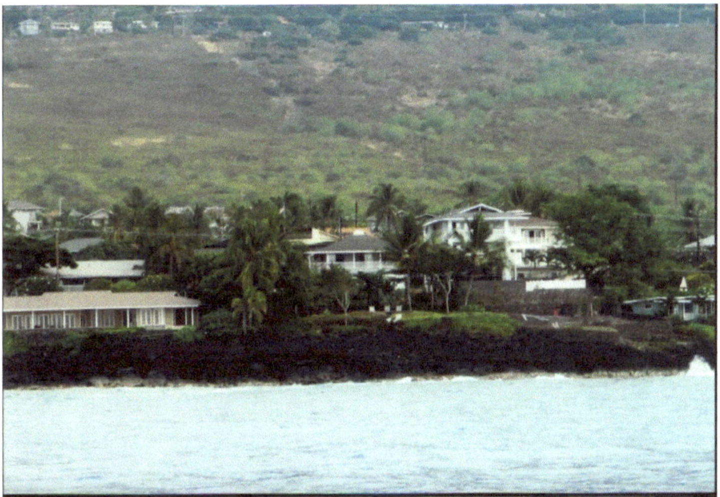

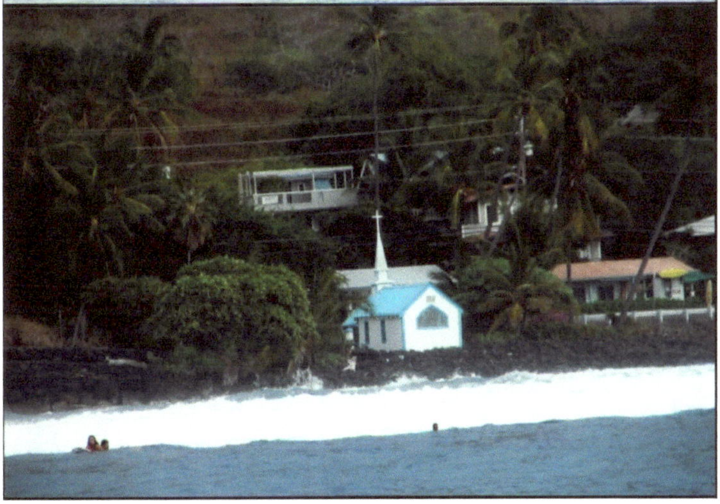

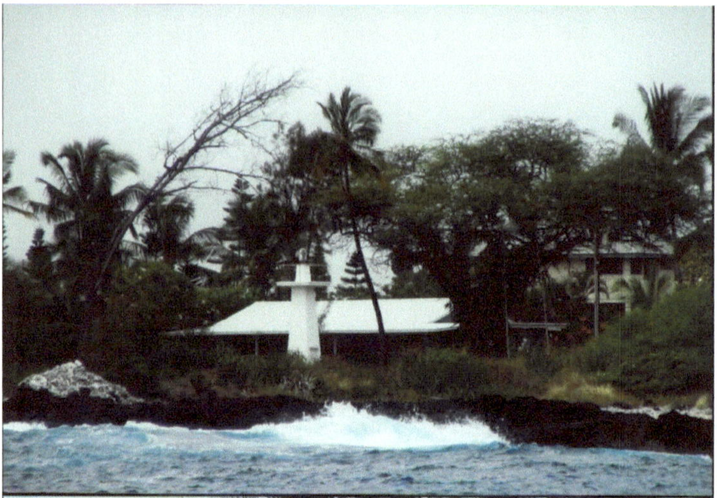

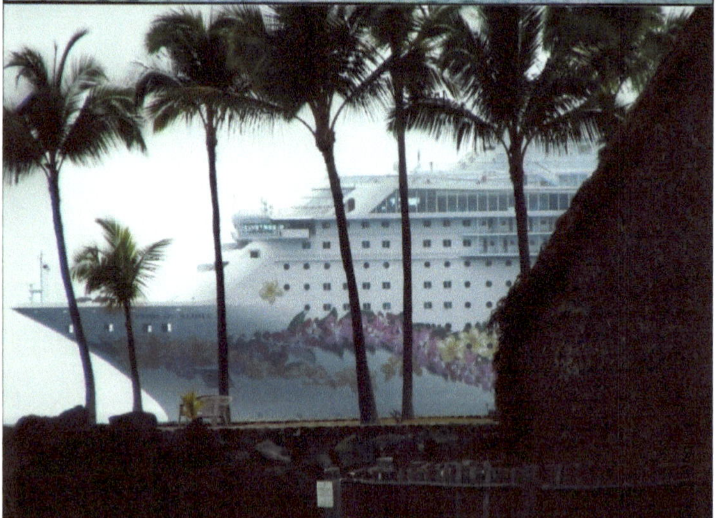

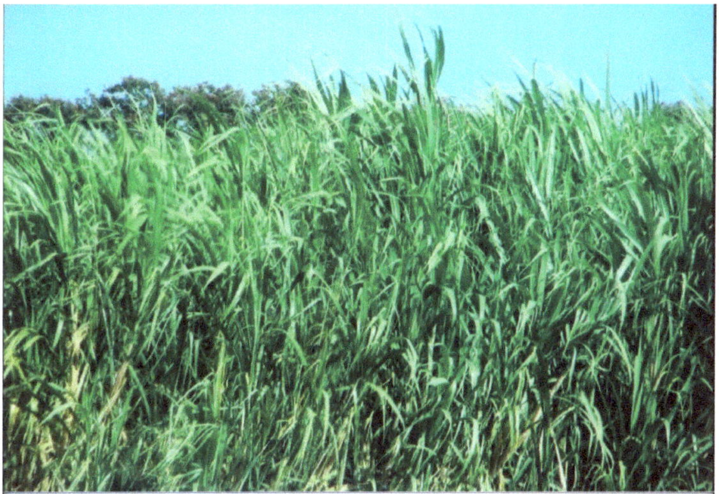

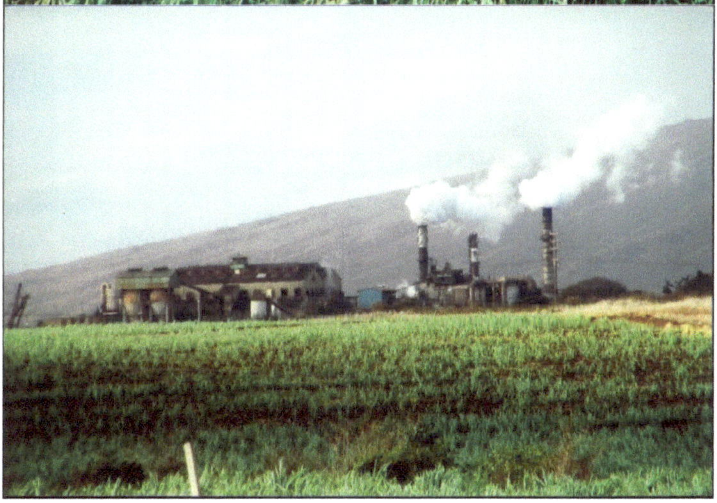

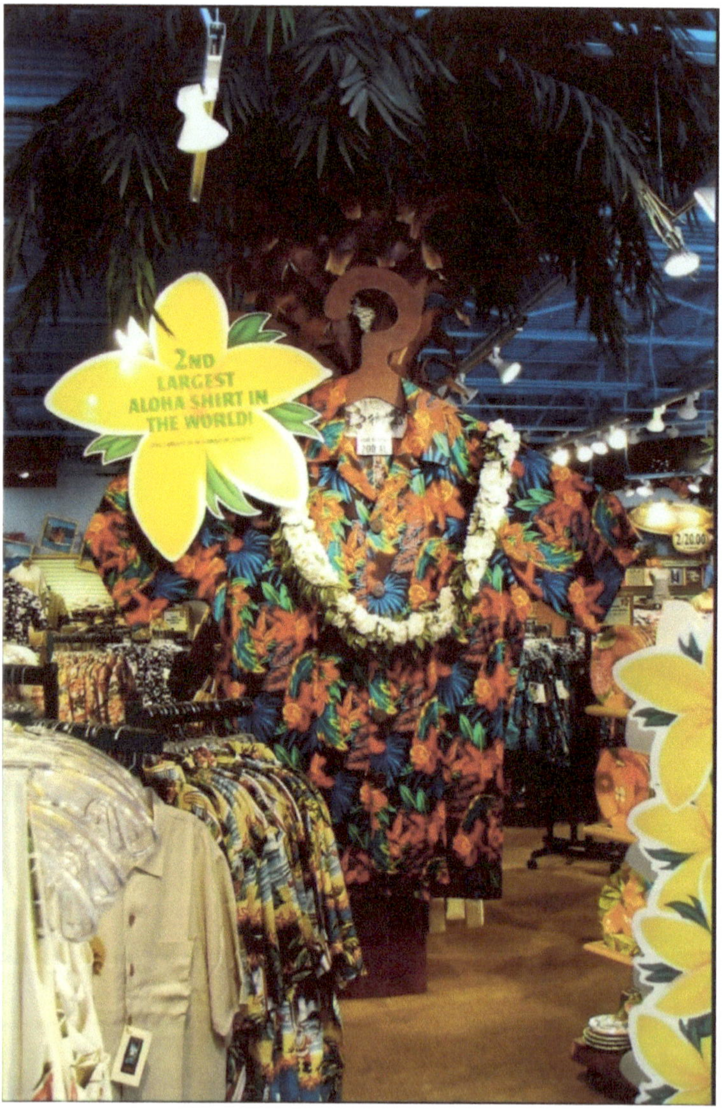
2ND
LARGEST
ALOHA SHIRT IN
THE WORLD!
2/20.00

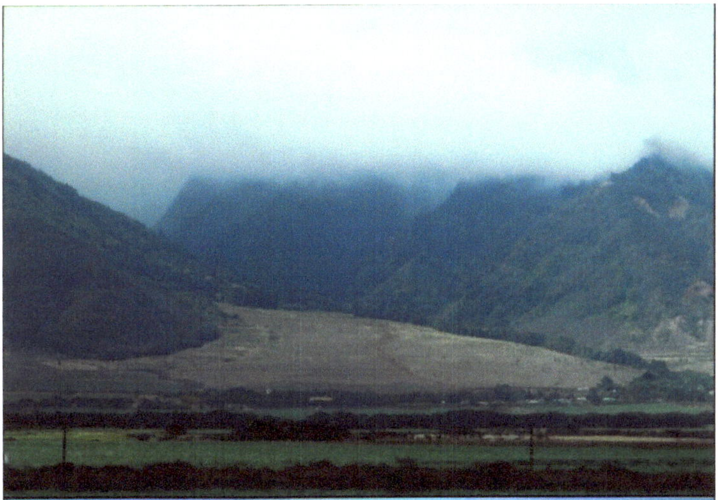

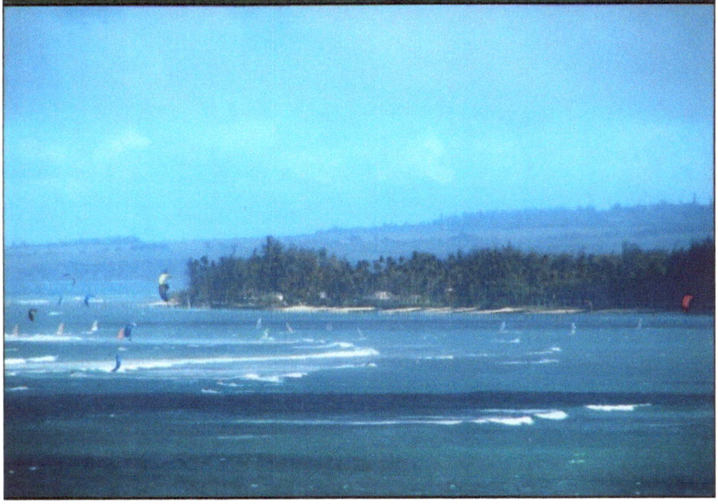

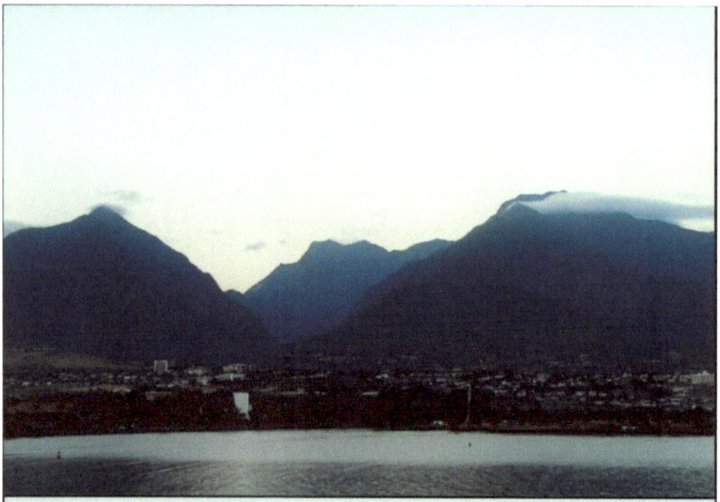

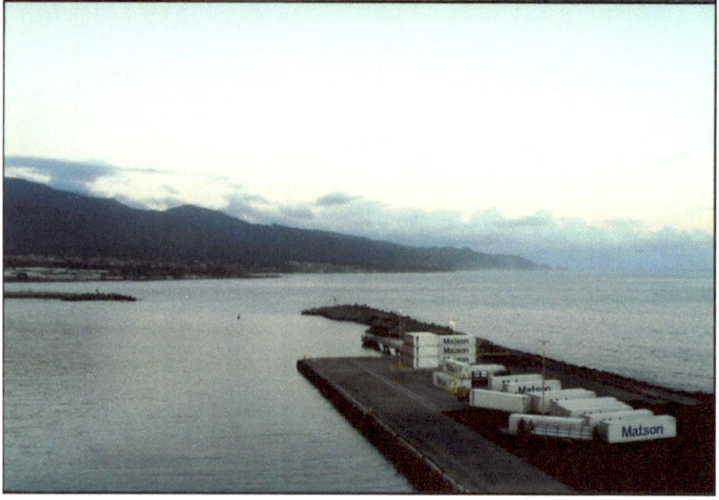
Matson

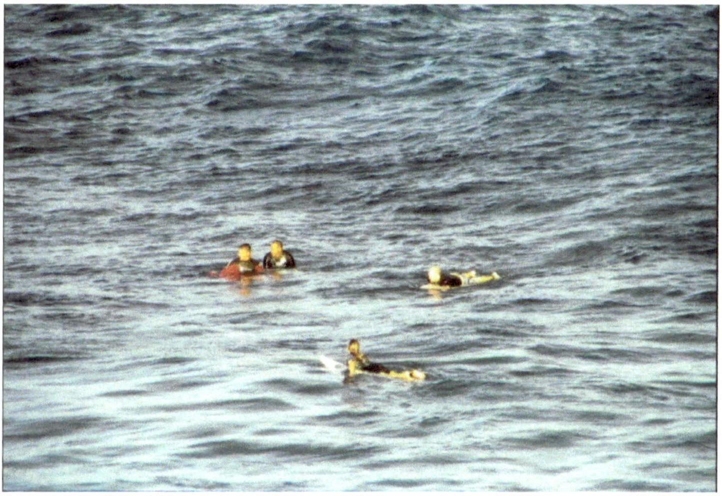

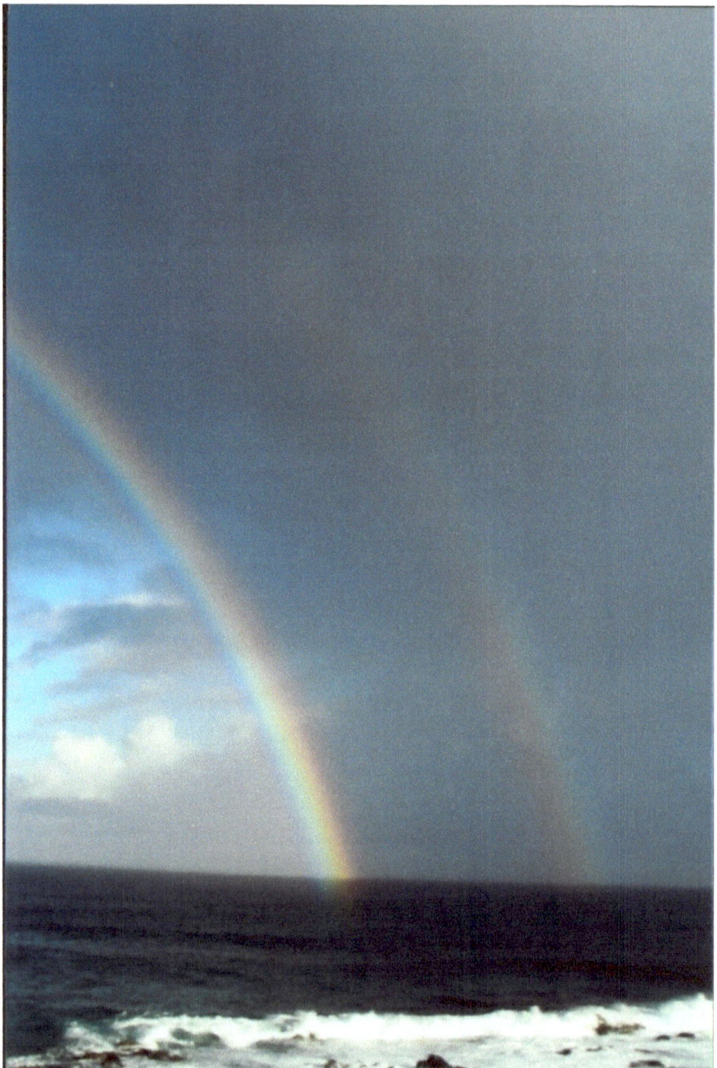

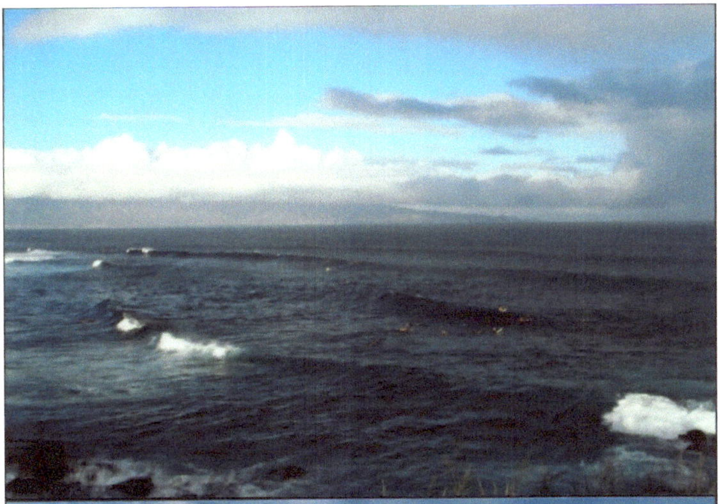

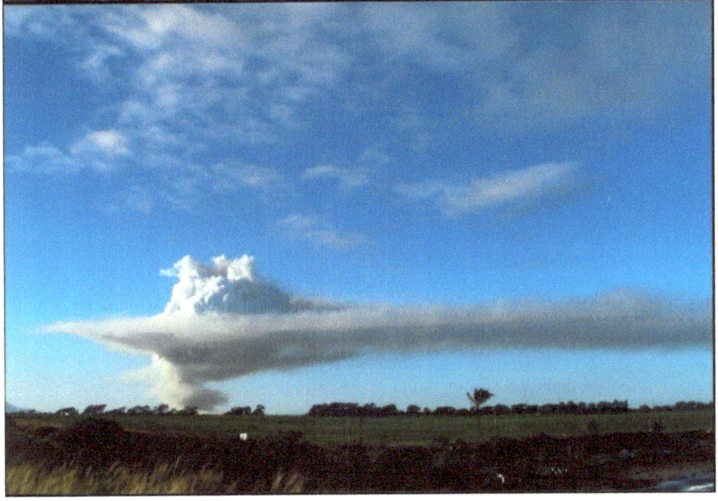

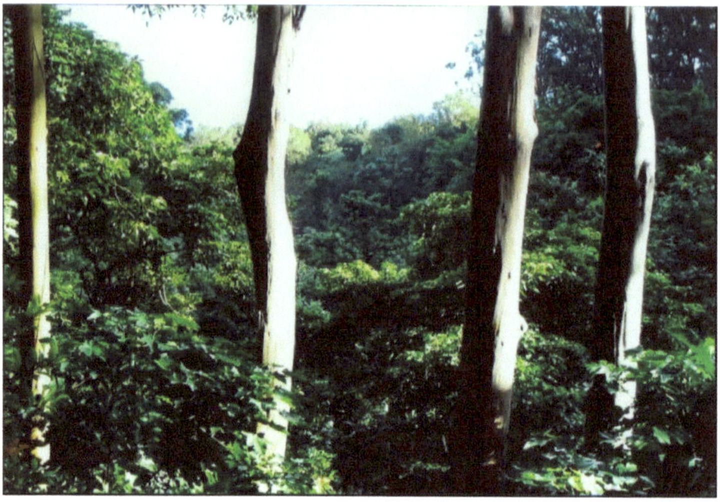

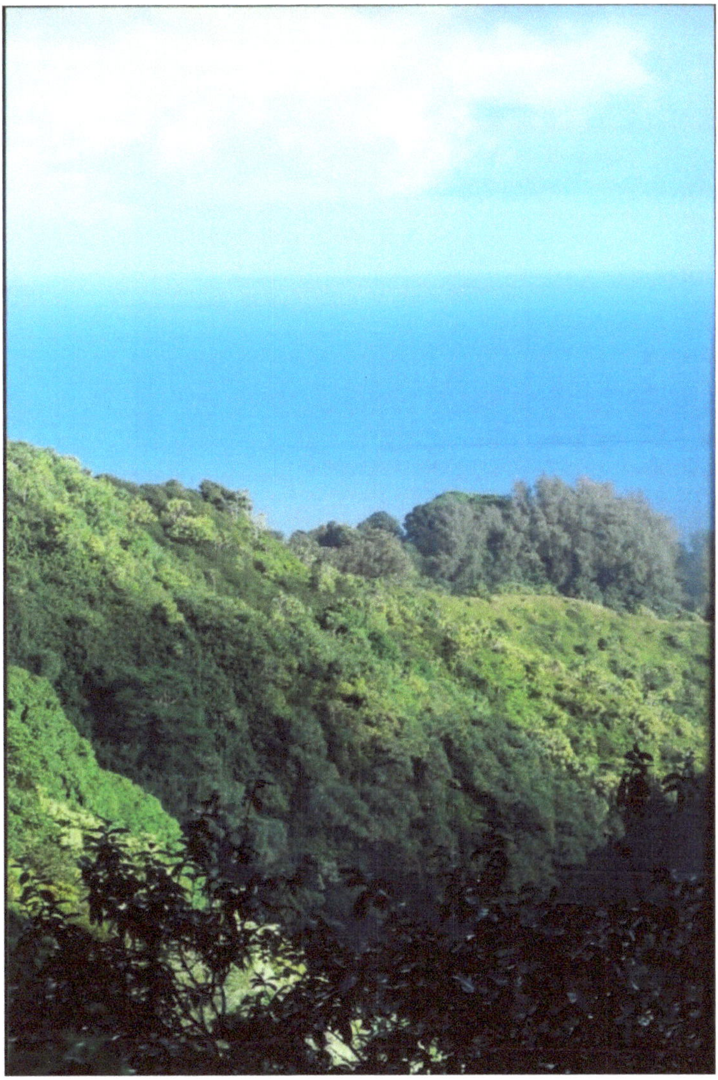

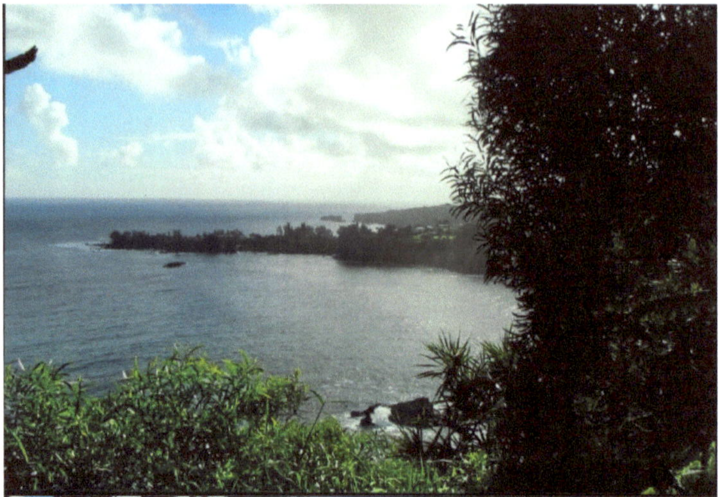
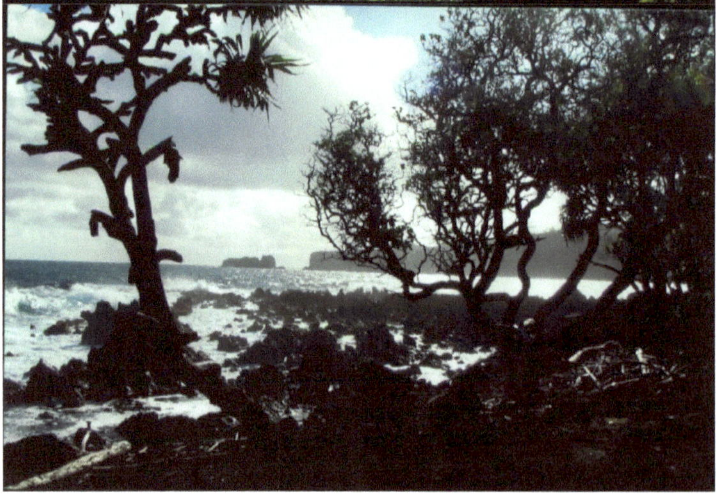

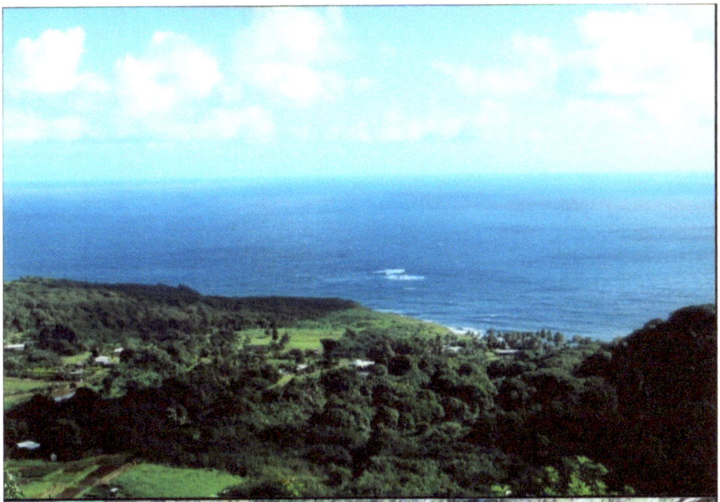

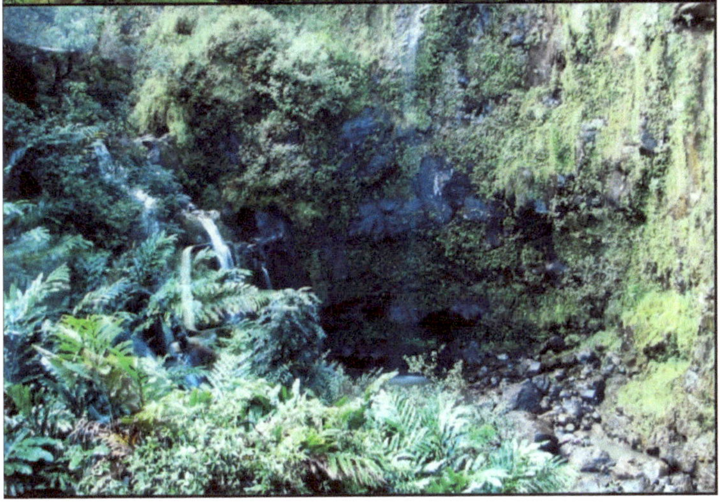

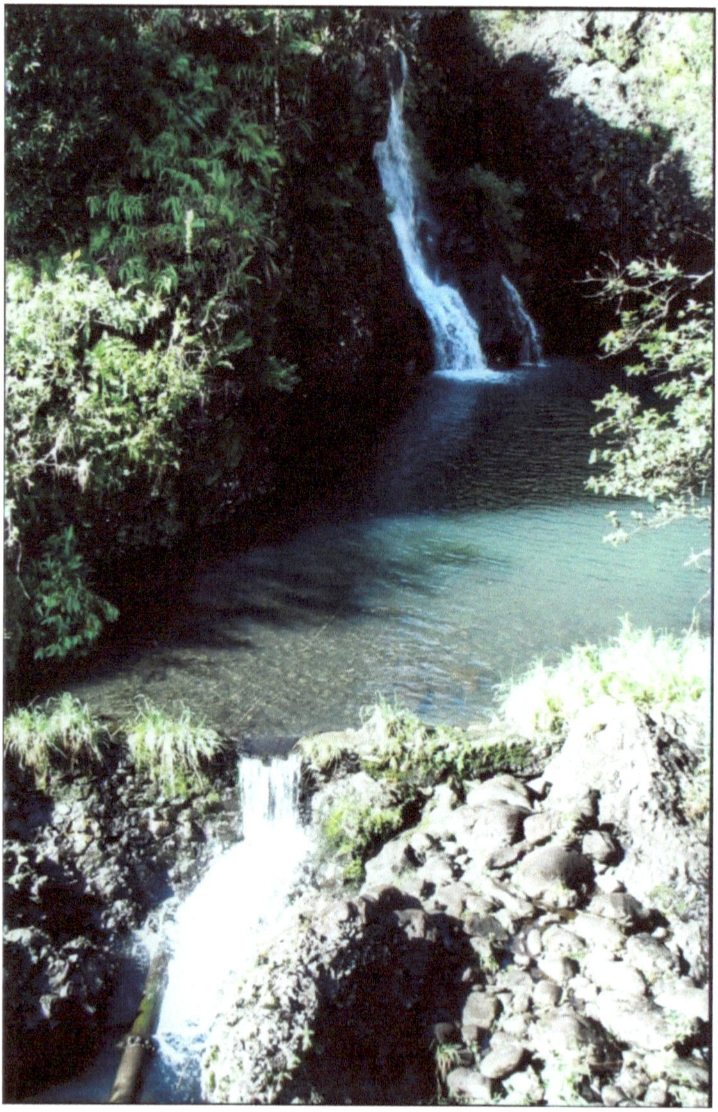

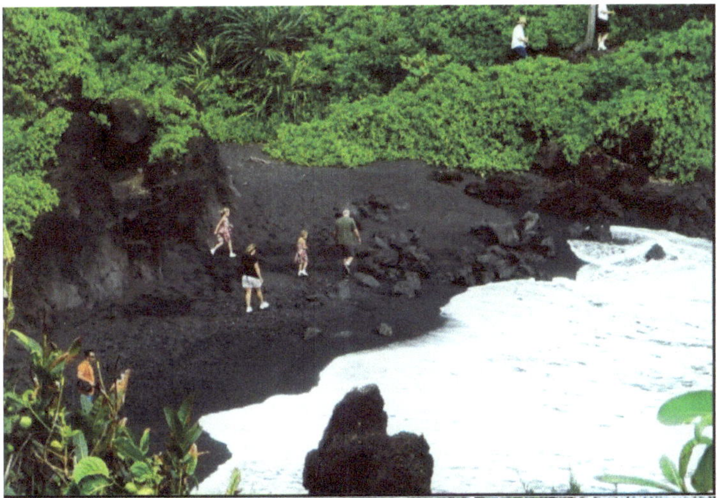
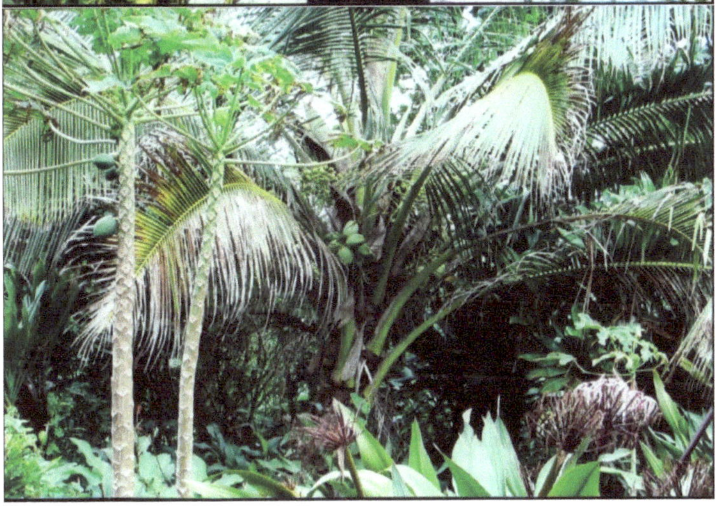

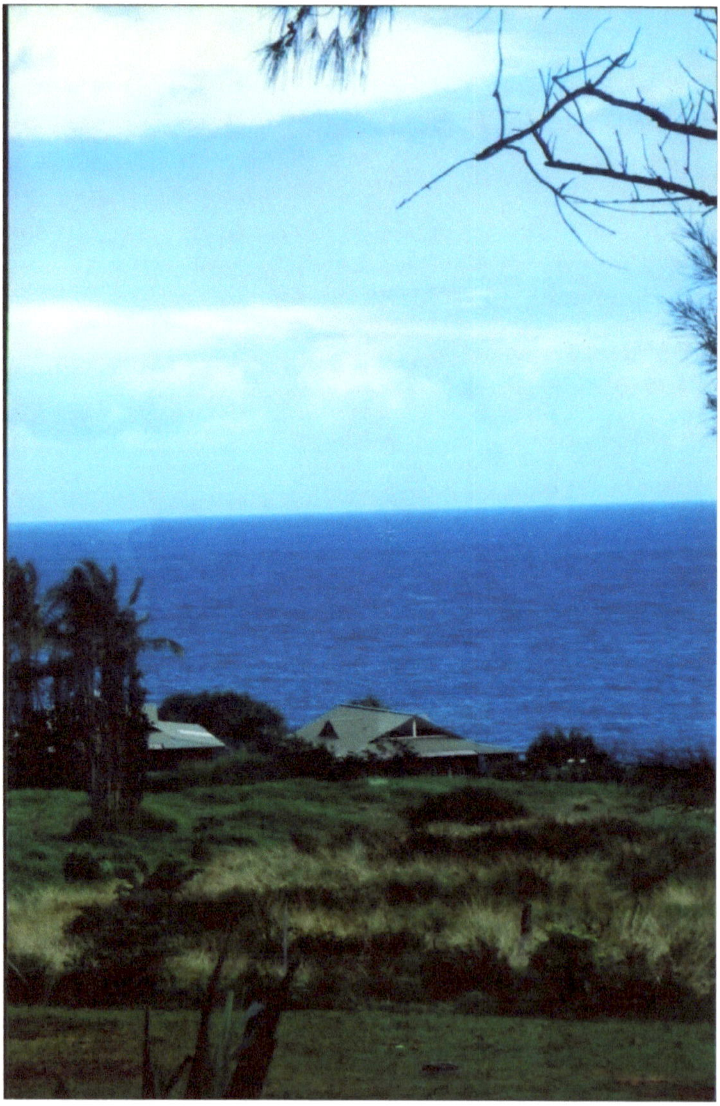

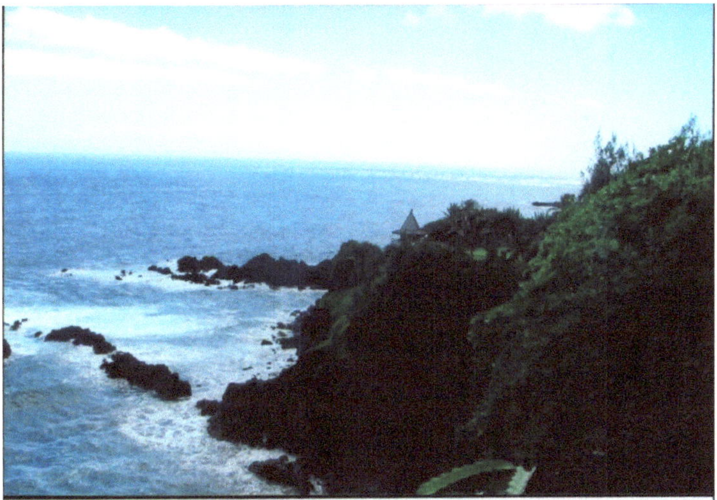

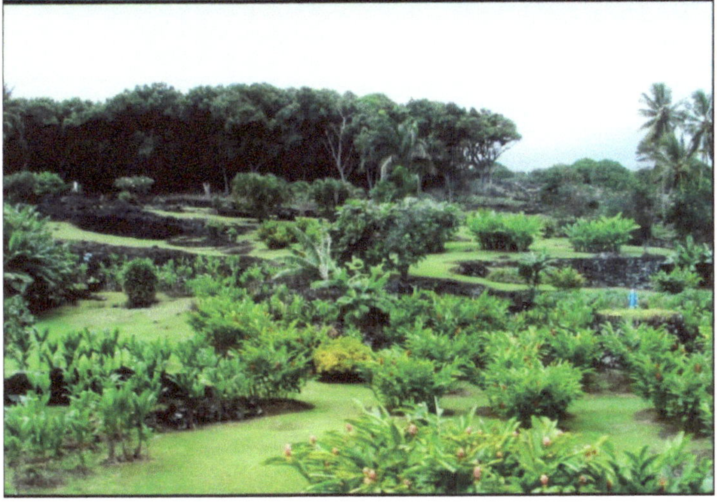

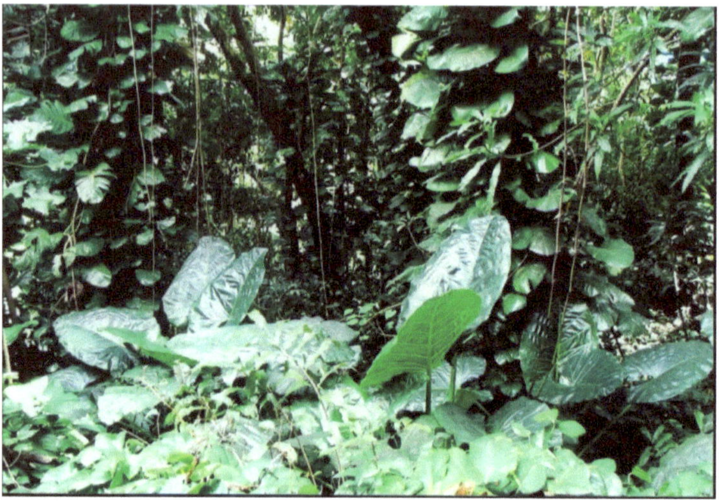

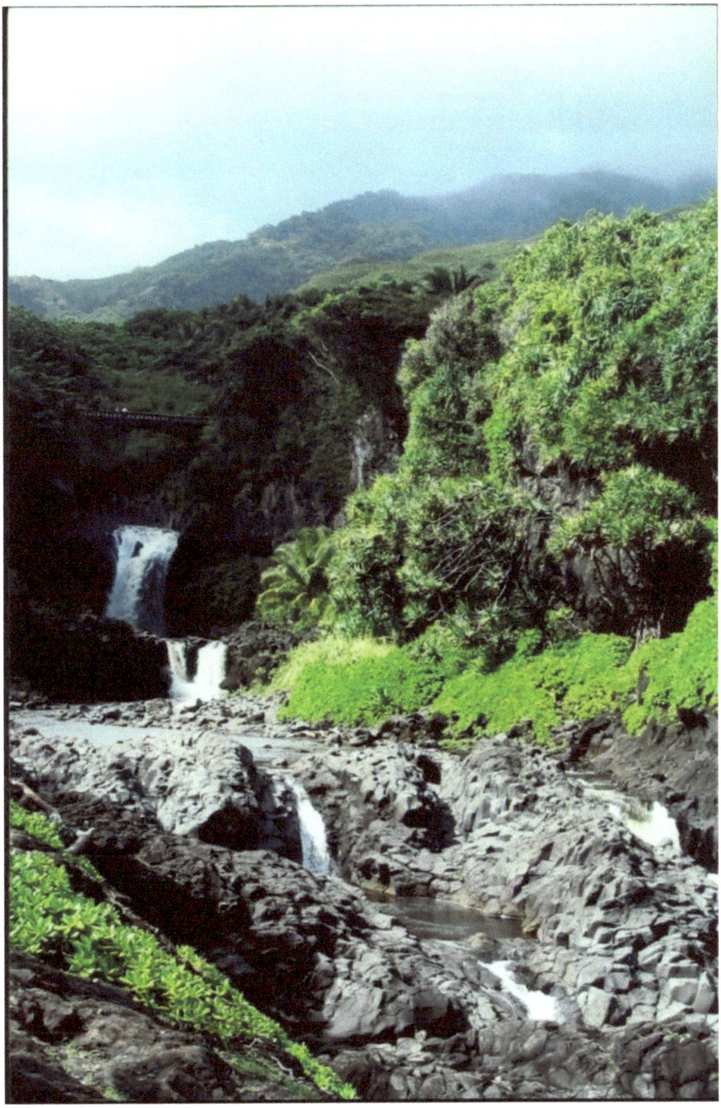

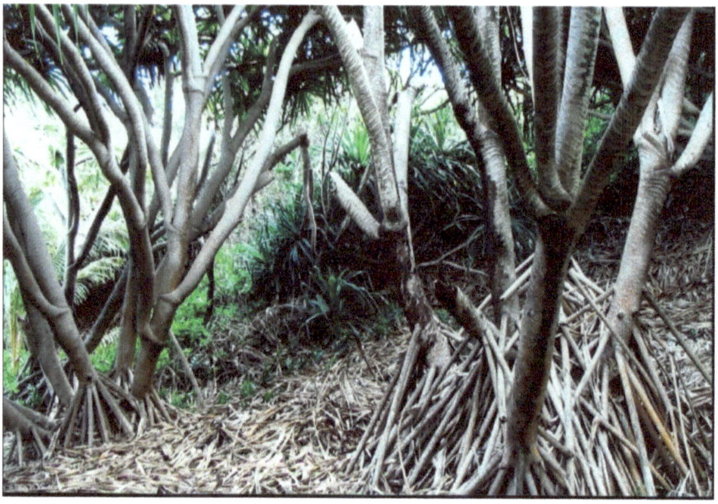

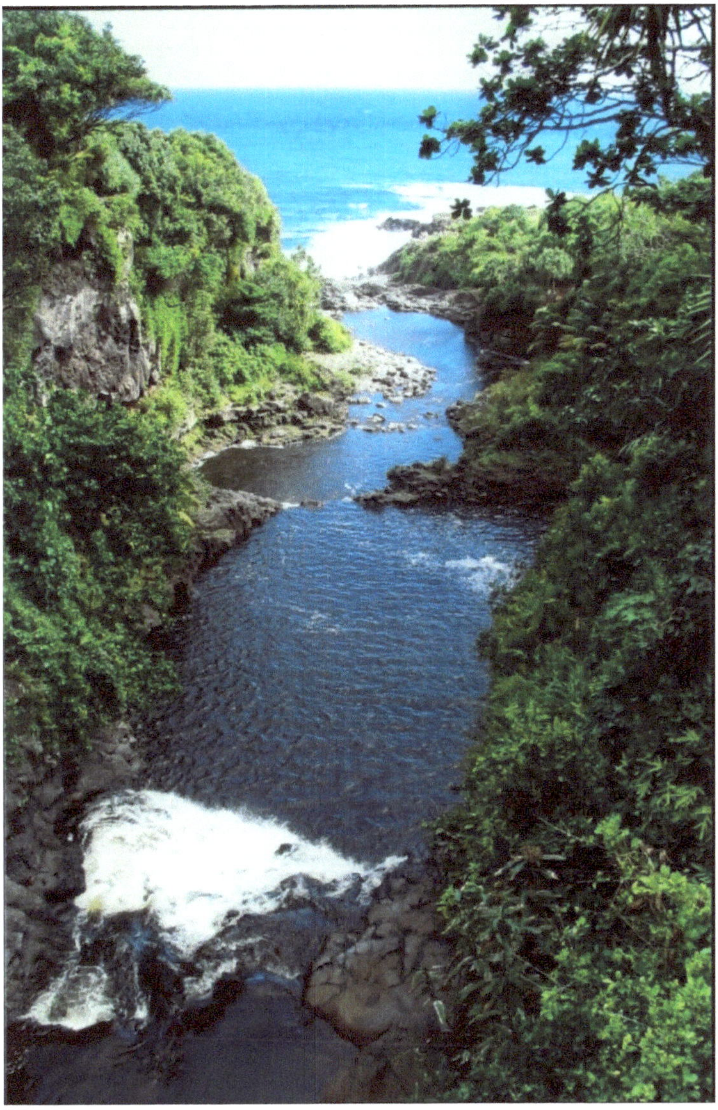

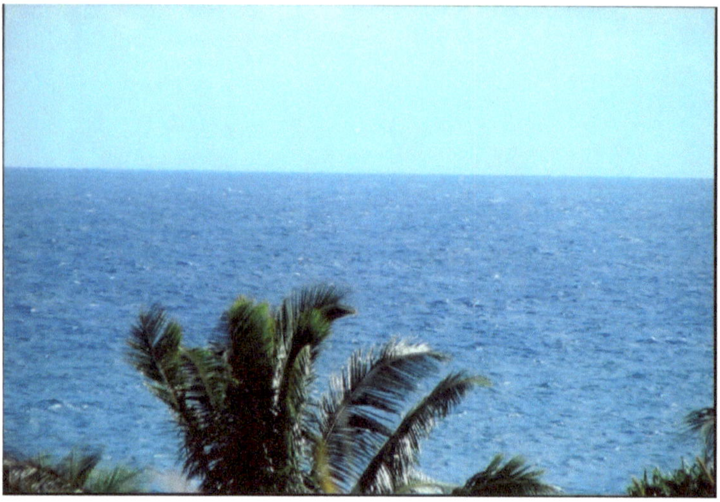

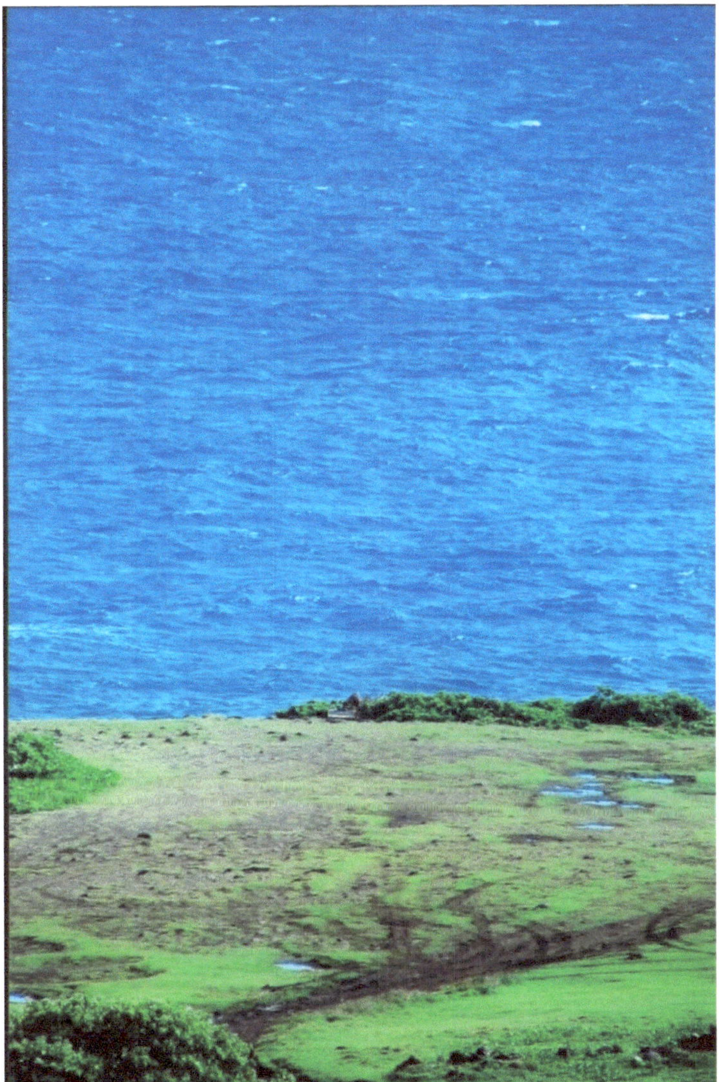

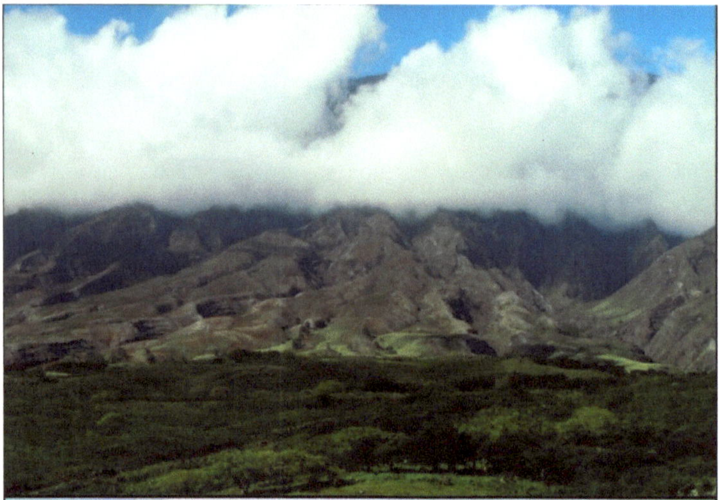

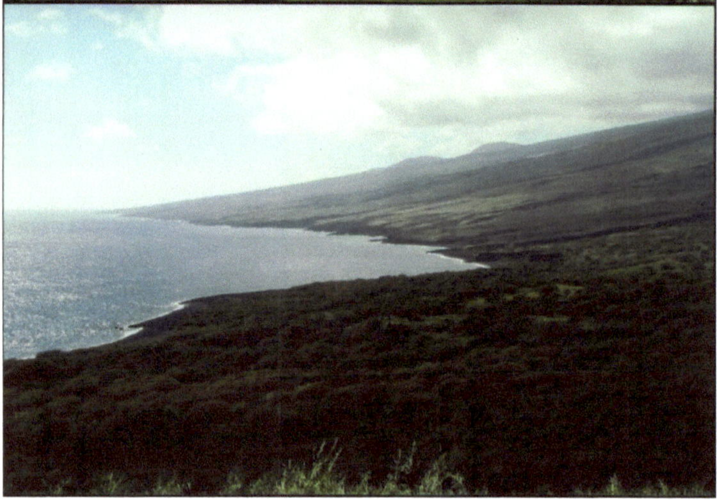

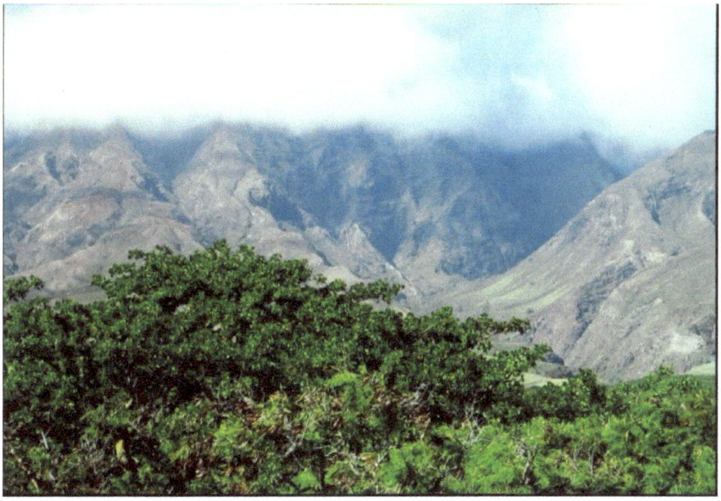

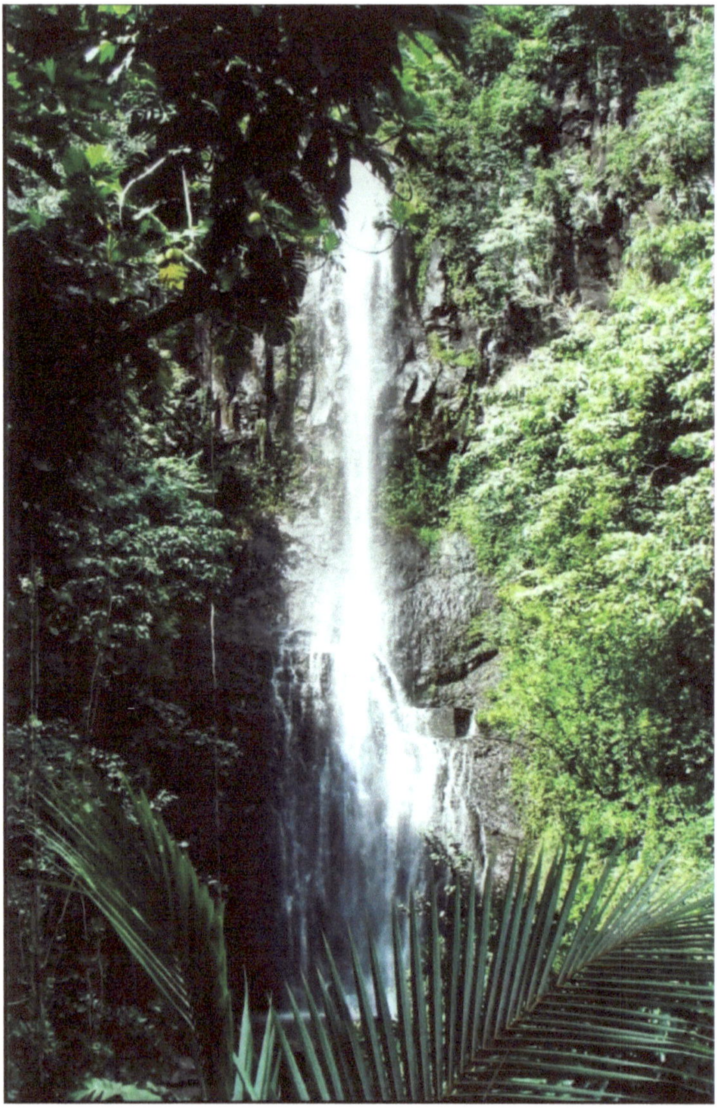

www.ingramcontent.com/pod-product-compliance
Lightning Source LLC
Chambersburg PA
CBHW040828180526
45159CB00001B/111
* 9 7 8 1 5 1 4 3 3 9 1 1 4 *